Read It Again!

MORE BOOK 1

A Guide for Teaching Reading through Literature

Terri Christman, M. Ed.
Liz Rothlein, Ed. D.

Illustrated by Sue Breitner

GoodYearBooks
An Imprint of ScottForesman
A Division of HarperCollins Publishers

I am dedicating this book, with much love, to Tom Wild. May you continue to always be the wind in my sail. —T.L.C.

To my friends, Martha Eisenhart and family in Interlaken, Switzerland, who have made my many visits there tranquil, creative, and inspiring. —L.C.R.

Good Year Books
are available for preschool through grade 6 for every basic curriculum subject plus many enrichment areas. For more Good Year Books, contact your local bookseller or educational dealer. For a complete catalog with information about other Good Year Books, please write:

Good Year Books
Scott, Foresman and Company
1900 East Lake Avenue
Glenview, IL 60025

GoodYearBooks
An Imprint of ScottForesman
A Division of HarperCollinsPublishers

CONTENTS

INTRODUCTION

Objectives

Read It Again! More Book 1 is designed to enable students to extend their enjoyment of quality literature as they develop vital thinking and learning skills. The activities in this book are offered as ways to help students meet the objectives for literature study developed by The National Council of Teachers of English (1983):

1. Realize the importance of literature as a mirror of human experience, reflecting human motives, conflicts, and values.
2. Be able to identify with fictional characters in human situations as a means of relating to others; gain insights from involvement with literature.
3. Become aware of important writers representing diverse backgrounds and traditions in literature.
4. Become familiar with masterpieces of literature, both past and present.
5. Develop effective ways of talking and writing about varied forms of literature.
6. Experience literature as a way to appreciate the rhythms and beauty of the language.
7. Develop habits of reading that carry over into adult life.

Applications

Read It Again! More Book 1 is an activity book brimming with imaginative teaching ideas for fifteen easily accessible, popular, and highly regarded children's books. Students in kindergarten through grade two will benefit from these materials. In addition to exposure to proven and well-loved stories, the activities in the book will help children to develop skills in word recognition, story comprehension, and process writing. There are activities that involve children in drawing, painting, puppetry, improvisation, geography, storytelling, mathematics and cooking. Critical thinking skills can be built by using the suggested discussion questions which reflect Boom's Taxonomy (1956).

Read It Again! More Book 1 can be adapted to almost any classroom setting. Chapter 1 and Resource Room teachers as well as librarians will find it useful, too. These activities, designed for a range of ability levels, can be used with large groups, small groups, or as independent work.

Read It Again! More Book 1 is also an excellent resource for parents. The suggested books and activities will help parents to develop their children's appreciation for literature as they encourage their children to develop the skills necessary to become effective and involved readers themselves.

Features

Background Information: *Read It Again! More Book 1* contains a selection of fifteen easy-to-find books with an established record of success as read-aloud books for children. Names of the author, illustrator and publisher as well as the publication date, number of pages and appropriate grade level are provided for each book.

Summary: A brief summary of each story is included for the convenience of teachers, librarians, and parents.

Introduction: A recommendation for introducing each story in a way that will capture children's interest and set the stage for reading is included.

Vocabulary: Key vocabulary words, along with motivating ways to present them, are included for each story.

Discussion Questions: Discussion questions to use during and after the reading of the stories are provided. These questions have been designed to foster higher level thinking skills.

Bulletin Boards: Ideas for creating interesting bulletin boards based on the selected books are described. Many of these bulletin boards call for the participation of the whole class and require minimal teacher direction.

Special Notes about the Activities: Explanations and instructions for the teacher about the use of individual activity sheets are included in this section when necessary.

Activity Sheets: Three reproducible activity sheets are provided for each selected book. Many of these activities can be used to correlate the language arts and literature curricula with other subject areas. Others are designed to develop language arts, reading and critical thinking skills. For flexibility and ease of use, the worksheets are arranged according to difficulty. Activity Sheet 1 is designed for use at the kindergarten level, Activity Sheet 2 is designed for use in first grade, and Activity Sheet 3 is for the second grade. However, all three may be used by one child: Activity Sheet 1 could be considered an independent activity, Activity Sheet 2 as an instructional activity, and Activity Sheet 3 as enrichment. Based on the ability and interests of the child, teachers and/or parents will determine which activities are most appropriate to meet individual needs.

Additional Activities: Additional book-related activities which involve children in study across the curriculum also are provided. Teachers can choose activities--focusing on varying skills and interests--for groups and/or individuals among several possibilities. At least one cooking activity is included for each of the selected books, too.

Vocabulary Listing: The Appendix contains a listing of all the vocabulary words introduced for the selected books.

Book Evaluation: A reproducible book evaluation form is included for children's use.

Concluding Activities: This section contains activity sheets that can be used after all the selected books in *Read It Again! More Book 1* have been introduced and read. These activities can be used as reproducibles or may be adhered to tagboard, laminated and used for independent learning center activities.

Additional Read-Aloud Books: Teachers and parents will find other quality read-aloud books listed in this bibliography.

Answer Key: Answers to several of the activity sheets are provided for the convenience of teachers and parents.

Guidelines for Using the Book

Before using the activities in *Read It Again! More Book 1*, it is important that the teacher and/or parent presents the selected books in an interesting and meaningful way. When sharing literature with young children, it is important that the children enjoy themselves as they develop skills that will be of benefit to them when they read on their own.

Reading aloud to children is an excellent way of instilling a love for literature. When reading aloud, the following suggestions may be helpful:

1. Establish a regular schedule for reading aloud.
2. Practice reading the book to acquaint yourself with the story before you present it to the child.
3. Create a comfortable atmosphere in which distractions are minimal.
4. Have a prereading session to set the stage for reading the book. Talk about the title and author/illustrator of the book, examine its cover and look at its introductory pages together, and set a purpose for reading.
5. Read with feeling and expression. Careful attention to pitch and stress is necessary if printed dialogue is to sound like conversation.
6. Hold the book so everyone can see the print as well as the illustrations.
7. Allow children to participate in the story when appropriate. They can place characters on a flannel board, move puppets when they "talk," and repeat rhyming words or refrains. Occasionally, you might want to stop and ask children what they think might happen next, or predict how the story may end.
8. Provide opportunities for children to respond to the story. Although not always necessary, it is often beneficial to do some follow-up activities involving discussion, dramatization, art, writing and further reading.

Children can also interact with books through a silent reading period, often referred to as Sustained Silent Reading (SSR). SSR provides children with an opportunity to read independently. The following suggestions may be helpful in setting up an SSR program in your classroom:

1. Provide the children with a wide selection of books from which to choose. Be sure to include those you have read aloud.
2. Allow time for the children to browse through the books and select a book to read.
3. Provide a regular time, each day, for SSR so that children can come to expect this period as a permanent part of their routine.
4. Start the program gradually with only two to five minutes at the outset. Gradually increase the time.
5. Make sure everyone reads, including the teacher and non-readers. Non-readers can "read" the illustrations.
6. It is important to continue a read-aloud program through the grades. Many of the books read aloud will later be selected by children to read independently.
7. Allow a time at the end of SSR for children to share what they have read. Ask questions such as: What is something interesting you read about today? What characters in the book you read did you like best? Why?

The flexible format of *Read It Again! More Book 1* allows the teacher or parent to use it in a variety of ways. The selected books and many of the activities can be presented in any order, although the following presentation to the children is suggested:

1. Introduce the selected book.
2. Read the book aloud.
3. Ask the discussion questions.
4. Introduce the vocabulary words. Follow by rereading the story, asking children to listen carefully for these words.
5. Put up the bulletin board.
6. Introduce the activity sheet(s).
7. Select additional activities/ideas.

The amount of time you spend on each book and the number and type of extension activities you select will depend on your schedule and the children's ages, abilities and interests. We hope you and your children will have fun and grow to love books as you *Read it Again*.

Bibliography

Bloom, B.S., M.B. Englehart, S.J. Furst, W.H. Hill, & D.R. Krathwohl. *Taxonomy of Educational Objectives. The Classification of Educational Goals. Handbook I: Cognitive Domain.* New York: Longmans Green, 1956.

National Council of English Teachers. "Essentials of English". *Language Arts*, Feb. 1983, Vol. 60, pp. 244–48.

SELECTED BOOKS AND ACTIVITIES

ALEXANDER AND THE WIND-UP MOUSE

Author
Leo Lionni

Illustrator
Leo Lionni

Publisher
Pantheon, 1969

Pages	Grade Level
30	K-3

Other Books by Lionni
Frederick; The Biggest House in the World; Fish Is Fish; Little Blue and Little Yellow; Pezzetino; Swimmy; It's Mine; Nadarian; Six Crows; Tico and the Golden Wings

Summary
Alexander, the mouse, is very lonely. Every time he comes out of his mouse hole, people scream and throw things. One day he meets Willy, a wind-up mouse that everyone loves. Alexander is envious, so Willy tells him about a magic lizard who can change one animal into another. But when the time for the change comes, Alexander doesn't want to become a wind-up mouse. Instead, he asks the lizard to turn Willy into a real mouse. The two friends are reunited in Alexander's mouse hole.

Introduction
Before beginning to read, show children the book's cover as well as one of the illustrations that shows both mice (the illustration of the two under the table next to the doll is especially suitable). Ask questions that will help children to look closely at both pictures. For example, ask: Are the mice big or little? How can you tell? (Children should observe how small the mice look in comparison to the doll and the table leg.) Does Alexander look like a real mouse? Why or why not? (Answers will vary.) How are Alexander and the wind-up mouse alike? (They are the same size and color.) How are they different? (Besides noting the key and wheels, help children to see that the wind-up mouse has a smooth outline; Alexander does not. Alexander's eyes are larger.) Encourage children to see if these similarities and differences can be found in the other illustrations throughout the book.

Key Vocabulary
After introducing and reading the story, write the following words on the chalkboard and choral read:

mouse	friends	magic	lizard
garden	pebble	house	moon

Give the students a copy of the following page. Ask the students to look at the correctly written words on the chalkboard as they unscramble the words on the worksheet. Then ask them to write the word correctly on the blank next to the scrambled word.

SCRAMBLED WORD WORKSHEET

Name_____ Date_____

1. lbbepe

2. nmoo

3. ardliz

4. mgaci

5. oushe

6. muoes

7. engrda

8. frendis

From *Read It Again! More Book 1*, published by Good Year Books. Copyright © 1991 Terri Christman and Liz Rothlein.

ALEXANDER AND THE WIND-UP MOUSE

Discussion Questions

1 Why do you think people screamed for help, threw things and chased Alexander with a broom when they saw him? (Answers may vary.)

2 How did Willy know that he was Annie's favorite toy? (She plays with him, she cuddles him, and at night he sleeps on a soft white pillow between a doll and a bear.)

3 Why did Alexander want to be like Willy? (He wanted to be cuddled and loved.)

4 Could the lizard make magic all the time? (Probably not.) How do we know? (He asked Alexander to come back, bringing a purple pebble, when the moon was round.)

5 What do you think the purple pebble Alexander found could be? (Answers may vary, but might include: a marble, a button, etc.)

6 Why do you think Alexander decided to change Willy from a wind-up mouse into a real mouse instead of changing himself into a wind-up mouse? (Answers may vary.)

7 If you knew a magic lizard, what animal would you ask him to change you into? (Answers may vary.)

Bulletin Board

Place white paper on bulletin board. Using many colors of construction paper, cut out the letters The Magic Lizard and adhere to the bulletin board. Place a moon in one of the top corners of the bulletin board. Give each student a copy of the lizard (printed on page 3); ask them to cut out the lizard and paint over it with a paintbrush dipped in water. Next, have them dip their brushes into different colors of paint and brush onto the lizard. The various colors will run together. Once their lizards have dried, have the children glue them onto an 8 1/2" x 11" piece of paper. underneath, have them complete the sentence: I would like the lizard to change me into _____. Students may want to add a circle cut from purple construction paper to their picture.

Special Notes about the Activities

Activity 2: This activity can be done as a group if children need special help with vocabulary or with filling in the chart. Answers may vary, and encourage children to talk about their reasons. The activity can be extended to a similar chart about Willy.

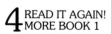

From *Read It Again! More Book 1*, published by Good Year Books. Copyright © 1991 Terri Christman and Liz Rothlein.

ALEXANDER AND THE WIND-UP MOUSE

ACTIVITY SHEET 1

Name_____ Date_____

Directions

Color the ◯ (moon) yellow.

Color the 〰 (grass) green.

Color the 🐁 (mouse) grey.

Color the ⬭ (pebble) purple.

Color the 🌳 (tree) brown.

Color the ☁ (sky) blue.

Color the 🦎 (lizard) red.

Name_____ Date_____

Directions
Put an X in the boxes under the words that tell how Alexander was feeling during one of these important parts of the story. The first one is done for you. (Hint: Sometimes you might want to use more than one X.)

story part	sad	afraid	worried	happy
People scream at Alexander.	X			
Alexander meets Willy.				
Alexander plays with Willy in Annie's room.				
Alexander wants to be like Willy.				
Alexander learns about the lizard.				
Alexander looks for a purple pebble.				
Alexander finds Willy in the box of old toys.				
Alexander finds Willy in his mouse hole.				

From *Read It Again! More Book 1*, published by Good Year Books. Copyright © 1991 Terri Christman and Liz Rothlein.

Name_____ Date_____

**ACTIVITY
SHEET 3**

Directions

The author, Leo Lionni, created a lizard in his story who could create magic with a purple pebble when the moon was full. Imagine that you are writing your own book about a magical character and answer the questions below.

Who would that character be? _____

_____

_____

What would your character need to make magic? _____

_____

_____

Where would your character live? _____

_____

_____

Who would come to your character for magic? Why? _____

_____

_____

Describe the magic that your character could do. _____

_____

_____

Draw your magical character.

ALEXANDER AND THE WIND-UP MOUSE

Additional Activities

1 Read the Aesop fable "The City Mouse and the Country Mouse" to your students. After sharing the story, compare the lives of the two mice by placing the words *country* and *city* on the chalkboard. Tell children that you are going to reread the story and that they should be listening for words that describe the city and the country. Write down their answers as they are given. Once the two lists are complete, have the students work together to help you write two paragraphs, one about the city and the other about the country. Choral read the paragraphs. As a culminating activity, children can dictate or write a third paragraph telling where they would like to live if they were a mouse. An illustration could accompany this paragraph.

2 Give each student a copy of the lizard on page 3. Then give each student small pieces of various colors of construction paper to cover the lizard. (Children could also cut their own small pieces.) Glue each piece so that it is touching (sometimes overlapping) the next piece. The students will be creating a mosaic lizard. It will look like the magic lizard seen and described in *Alexander and the Wind-up Mouse.*

3 Give each student a tongue depressor, gray construction paper, and approximately twelve inches of black yarn. On one end of the tongue depressors, students should draw two eyes and a nose. Cut out two small gray circles for the mouse's ears. Glue the ears above the eyes on the tongue depressor. Next, cut six one-inch pieces of black yarn. Glue three of these pieces of yarn on each size of the nose on the tongue depressor. Finally, glue a six-inch piece of yarn on the other end of the tongue depressor for the tail. When completed, the student will have a bookmark or a puppet.

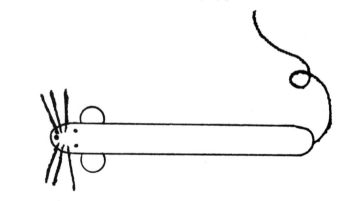

4 Draw children's attention to the illustrations in the book. They are done in collage. Leo Lionni used cut and torn paper to create the mice and the setting. Children can experiment with collage by creating their own mice out of cut or torn paper. They might want to add other details to their collage, too, just as the artist did.

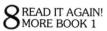

From *Read It Again! More Book 1*, published by Good Year Books. Copyright © 1991 Terri Christman and Liz Rothlein.

ALEXANDER
AND THE
WIND-UP
MOUSE

5 Students can create a mouse scene with their fingers. They will need a 5" x 8" index card and inked stamp pad. The students will press their fingers on the pad and then transfer it to their card. Once they have made the print, add the eyes, ear, nose, whiskers, a tail, and background scenery. They may want to turn their card over and write about their creation.

6 Contact a local pet store. Invite the owner to bring a pet mouse into the classroom for your students to see and touch. In preparation of the pet store visitor, have your students write down questions they will want to ask this person. Provide ample time for questions and touching.

An Extra Treat

Alexander's Cheese Delights

2 slices of bread for each student
2 slices of cheese for each student
butter
tinfoil
oil

Have students create their own grilled cheese sandwiches. Each student will need two slices of bread. They need to butter the outside of each slice of bread. Next, have them place slices of cheese on the bread. Wrap the cheese sandwich in tinfoil. Then iron both sides of the tinfoil (1 to 2 minutes on each side). Unwrap and enjoy.

THE BIGGEST BEAR

Author
Lynd Ward

Illustrator
Lynd Ward

Publisher
Houghton Mifflin, 1952

Pages	Grade Level
80	1-3

Other Books by Ward
The Silver Pony; Nic of the Woods; I Am Eyes—Ni Macho

Summary
Johnny decides to go looking for the biggest bear in the woods to shoot so he can have a bearskin on his barn like all the neighbors. He finds a bear cub and, instead of killing it, he brings it home. As the cub grows, it gets into more and more trouble. Johnny brings the bear back to the woods again and again, but the bear always comes back. Finally, Johnny is told to shoot him, but just as he is loading his gun, the bear smells maple sugar and runs after it. The maple sugar is the bait for an animal trap which snares both the bear and Johnny. The men who set the trap rescue them and the bear is taken to the zoo. Johnny promises the bear that he will visit often and bring maple sugar.

Introduction
Johnny was ashamed because there was a bearskin hanging on everybody's barn but his. He went looking for a big bear to shoot, but instead came home with a bear cub. Can you imagine how a bear would get along on a farm...especially if it grew to be a big bear? What kind of trouble do you think a bear could get into on a farm? How would the other animals like to have a big bear around? (Prompt with more questions if necessary.) Let's see if any of you could predict what happens in the story.

Key Vocabulary
After reading the story, write the following words on the chalkboard and choral read them.

valley	maple	gun	kill
orchard	cub	woods	bear

Key Vocabulary Instruction
Give each child a copy of the worksheet containing the scrambled words on page 11. Ask the children to look at the words written correctly on the chalkboard as they unscramble the words on the worksheet. Tell them to write the word correctly on the blank next to the scrambled word.

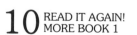
From *Read It Again! More Book 1*, published by Good Year Books. Copyright © 1991 Terri Christman and Liz Rothlein.

Name _____ Date _____

SCRAMBLED WORD WORKSHEET

1. reba

2. odows

3. ubc

4. adrocrh

5. pmlae

6. lilk

7. ung

8. yvlale

THE BIGGEST BEAR

Discussion Questions

1 Do you think Johnny would have wanted a bearskin hanging on his barn if his neighbors didn't have one? Explain. (Answers may vary.)

2 Johnny went hunting for a bear to kill so he could have a bearskin. What did he do when he found his first bear? (He gave it maple sugar and brought it home.)

3 Why do you think Johnny didn't shoot the bear cub the first time he saw it? (Answers may vary.)

4 What did it mean in the story when neighbors said the bear "was a trial and tribulation to the whole valley?" (Answers may vary.)

5 What did the bear do that made his neighbors upset? (He ate their food, e.g., corn, ham, maple syrup.)

6 Johnny's father told him to shoot the bear. How do you think you would feel if you had to do what Johnny had to do? (Answers may vary.)

7 Why do you think Johnny had a hard time putting the bullet in the gun? (Answers may vary but may include that he didn't want to shoot the bear.)

8 Do you think Johnny was glad that his bear finally ended up at the zoo? Why or why not? (Answers may vary.)

Bulletin Board

A bear is a very unusual pet. Discuss other animals that would be unusual pets. Ask the students to select an unusual animal they would like as a pet and draw a picture of it. Label the bulletin board, "MY UNUSUAL PET" and adhere the children's illustrations to the board.

From *Read It Again! More Book 1*, published by Good Year Books. Copyright © 1991 Terri Christman and Liz Rothlein.

THE
BIGGEST
BEAR

Name_____ Date_____

**ACTIVITY
SHEET 1**

Directions
Follow the dots 1-20 to make the picture below.
Then do the following:

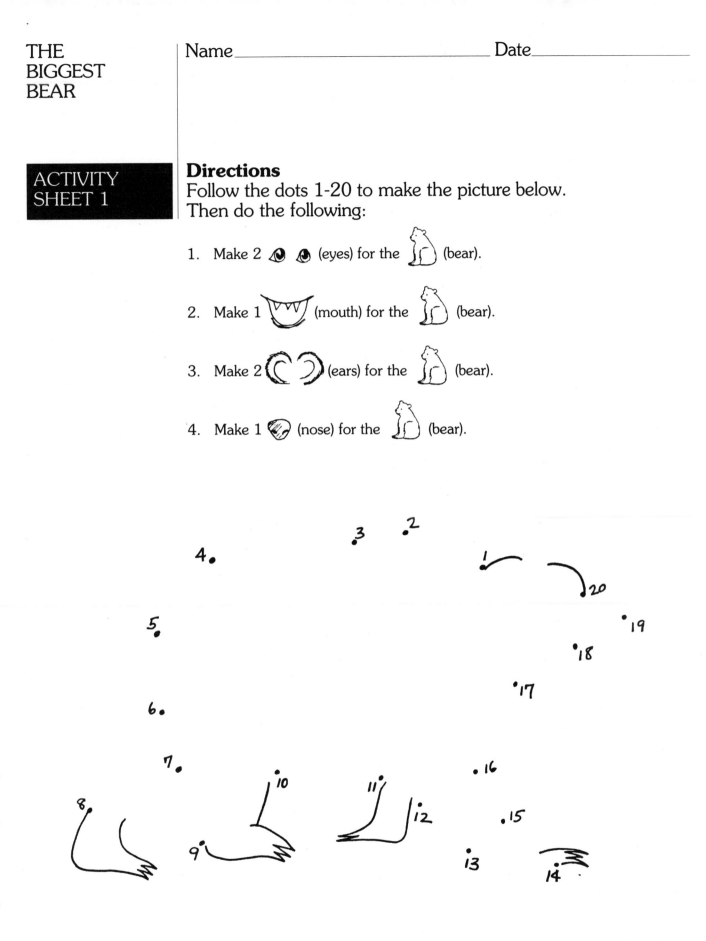

1.   Make 2 🦅 🦅 (eyes) for the 🐻 (bear).

2.   Make 1 〰️ (mouth) for the 🐻 (bear).

3.   Make 2 〰️ (ears) for the 🐻 (bear).

4.   Make 1 🌰 (nose) for the 🐻 (bear).

Name _____   Date _____

Directions

Follow the directions below:

1. Color the biggest bear brown.

2. Color the smallest bear black.

3. Color the middle-sized bear white.

4. Put an X under the bucket of maple syrup.

5. Draw a hat on the bear with two ears.

6. Put a ✝ to the left of the biggest bear.

7. Put two •• on the top of the middle-sized bear.

8. Put a ○ on the right of the biggest bear.

Name_____ Date_____

Directions

Johnny tried to leave his bear at four different places. Read the phrase in each box and draw a picture of the place. Then, put numbers in the paw patterns to show where Johnny went the first, second, third, and fourth times.

NORTH

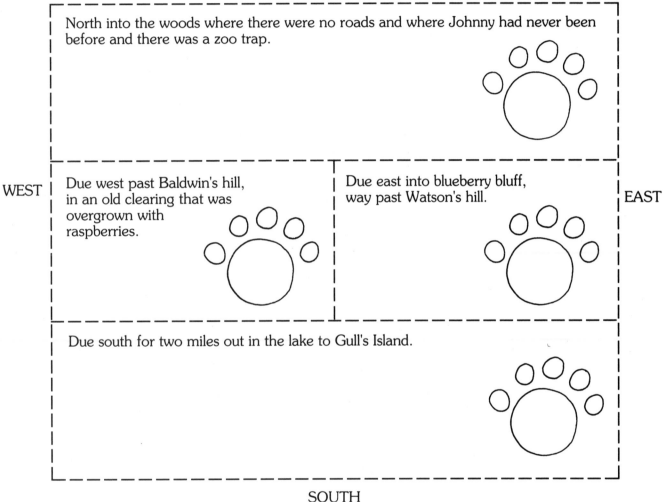

North into the woods where there were no roads and where Johnny had never been before and there was a zoo trap.

WEST

Due west past Baldwin's hill, in an old clearing that was overgrown with raspberries.

Due east into blueberry bluff, way past Watson's hill.

EAST

Due south for two miles out in the lake to Gull's Island.

SOUTH

THE BIGGEST BEAR

Additional Activities

1 In the story *The Biggest Bear,* Johnny took his bear back into the woods in many different directions: east, west, north, and south. Build an understanding of direction with activities such as the following. a) Label the classroom with signs indicating each of the directions. b) Show the students a map and point out the directions to them. c) Provide the students with activities in which they are involved in learning and/or reinforcing the concept of east, west, north, and south. For example, have them find a state that is east of Ohio, west of Colorado, etc. d) In the classroom or in gym, ask them to jump three times to the east, take four steps to the south, etc.

2 Talk with the children about all of the different foods that Johnny's bear ate in the story, e.g., maple sugar, mash, corn, pancakes, etc. List these foods on the chalkboard. Bring in a factual account of bears from an encyclopedia or another informational book and share it with children. What foods do bears living in woods eat? Make another list on the chalkboard. Compare the two lists. Are any foods the same?

3 Create a webbing with the word bear. The web should include places where a bear might be found, colors, foods, types, etc.

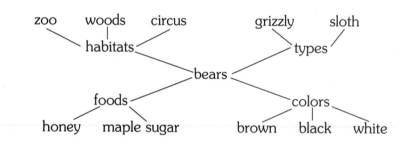

4 Create a "Teddy Bear Day" in which the children bring in their stuffed bears. Allow time for the children to share their bears. Provide books and conduct a read-aloud time using books such as *Beady Beare, Corduroy, Bearymore,* and *Pocket for Corduroy* by Don Freeman; *Blueberries for Sal* by Robert McCloskey; *Little Bear* by Else Homelund; or *The Three Bears* by Paul Galdone.

An Extra Treat

Provide an electric skillet, pancake mix, and hot plate. Make miniature pancakes for the class following the recipe on the box. Create maple syrup by mixing together the following:

> 2 cup water
> 2 tbsp. dark brown sugar
> 2 tsp. maple flavoring

Heat water until it boils. Lower heat and add the sugar. Cook over low heat until the sugar dissolves.

From *Read It Again! More Book 1,* published by Good Year Books. Copyright © 1991 Terri Christman and Liz Rothlein.

CAPS FOR SALE

Author
Esphyr Slobodkina

Illustrator
Esphyr Slobodkina

Publisher
Addison-Wesley, 1940

Pages	Grade Level
42	K-3

Other Books by Slobodkina
No other books are known by this author.

Summary
A peddler sells the caps he carries on his head for fifty cents a piece. One day he is unable to sell any caps, so instead, he walks into the country and takes a nap. While he is asleep, monkeys take his caps, climb up a tree, and place them on their heads. When the peddler wakes up, he tries to find a way to get his caps back from the monkeys.

Introduction
Ask the children to look at the cover of *Caps for Sale*. Then ask them: What do you see on the cover? What do you think the man, his caps, the tree, and the monkey have to do with each other?

Key Vocabulary
Write the following words on the chalkboard and choral read them.

peddler	tree	town	angry
caps	country	monkeys	head

Key Vocabulary Instruction
Draw a tree with eight branches on the chalkboard. Ask a student to select a vocabulary word and pronounce it. Once the student has pronounced it , have him or her write the word on a branch. Once the tree is full of the vocabulary words, choral read the words again.

CAPS
FOR
SALE

Discussion Questions

1 Why didn't anyone buy a cap from the peddler? (Answers may vary.)

2 Have you ever seen a peddler? If so, what was he/she selling? (Answers may vary.)

3 This peddler carried the caps he was selling on his head. How is he different from someone who sells caps in a store. (Answers may vary.)

4 Why did the peddler take a nap? (Answers may vary but might include: he was hungry, tired, couldn't sell caps.)

5 Why was the peddler so angry at the monkeys? (They took his caps and wouldn't give them back.)

6 If you were a peddler, what would you carry and sell? (Answers may vary.)

7 Describe the way the peddler always stacked his caps. (Checked cap, a bunch of gray caps, a bunch of brown caps, a bunch of blue caps, and, on the very top, a bunch of red caps.)

Bulletin Board

Place the caption, *Caps for Sale*, on the bulletin board. Photocopy the cap pattern below so that each student has a cap. Have the students design their cap using crayons, markers, glitter, construction paper, feathers, sequins, etc. Adhere their caps to the bulletin board.

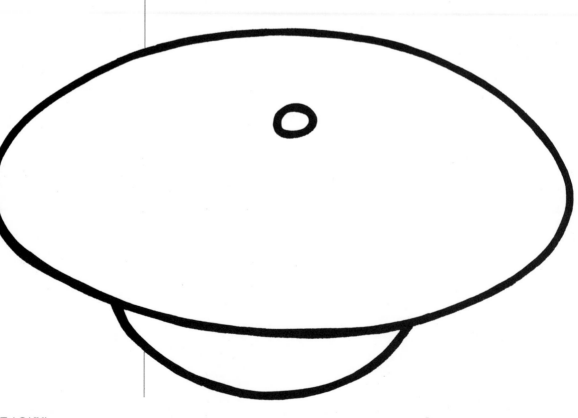

From *Read It Again! More Book 1*, published by Good Year Books. Copyright © 1991 Terri Christman and Liz Rothlein.

CAPS
FOR
SALE

ACTIVITY
SHEET 1

Directions

Below are some of the peddler's caps. Count the dots on each cap. Write the number on this line. Color the caps black and white, gray, brown, blue and red. They will look just like the peddler's!

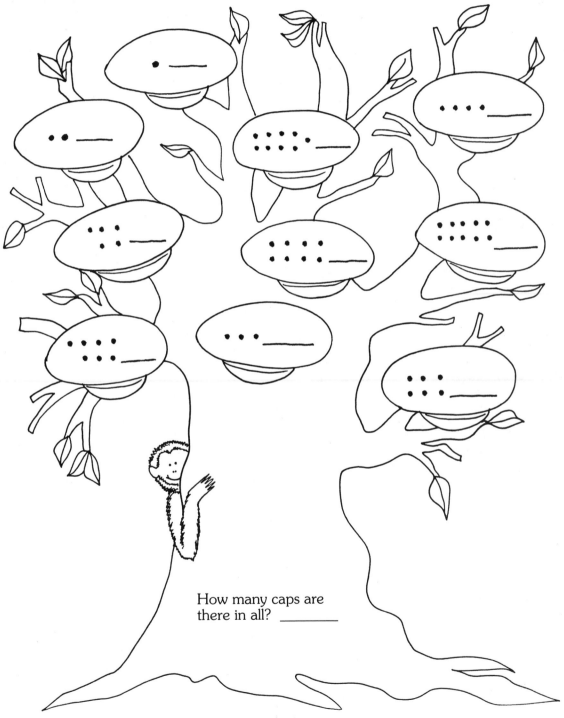

How many caps are
there in all? _____

Name_____ Date_____

Directions
Fill in the blanks below with the vocabulary words in the box.

1. town	3. tree	5. peddler	7. angry
2. caps	4. country	6. monkeys	8. head

Once upon a time there was a _____ who sold caps. He carried his

caps on his _____. He had his own checkered cap, then a bunch of gray

caps, then a bunch of brown caps, then a bunch of blue caps, and on the very

top a bunch of red caps.

One day, he could not sell any caps in _____. So, he walked out

into the _____. There he went to sleep under a _____. When

he woke up, his caps were missing. He looked up into the tree and saw

_____ wearing his caps. He was so _____. He spoke to

them, shook his finger at them, and stamped his feet at them. But everything

he did, they did. Finally he threw his cap on the ground and when he did this,

the monkeys did too. He picked up all the caps and went back to town calling,

"Caps! Caps for sale! Fifty cents a cap!"

From *Read It Again! More Book 1*, published by Good Year Books. Copyright © 1991 Terri Christman and Liz Rothlein.

Name_____ Date_____

From *Read It Again! More Book 1*, published by Good Year Books. Copyright © 1991 Terri Christman and Liz Rothlein.

**ACTIVITY
SHEET 3**

Directions

Tell us how you would be a successful peddler. _____

_____

If you were a peddler, what would you sell? _____

_____

What would it be like? _____

_____

What would you charge for what you are selling? _____

Where would you sell it? _____

_____

In the box below, draw yourself as a peddler.

CAPS FOR SALE

Additional Activities

1 Bring in a tree branch and place it in a pot filled with rocks. (Rocks will help secure the branch.) Invite each student to bring in a cap from home to hang on the tree. Ask children to tell or write about their caps: where did they get them? when do they wear them? are they special? how old are they? etc.

2 In this story, the monkeys do everything the peddler does. When he shakes his finger at them, they shake their fingers back at the peddler, when he shakes both hands at them, they shake their hands at the peddler. When he stamps his feet at them, they stamp their feet at the peddler. When he throws his cap on the ground, they throw their caps on the ground. Have a student come to the front of the room and create an action the students can mimic back. Continue until each student has a turn.

3 Have the students think about the many kinds of hats. List their suggestions on the chalkboard. Next, ask children to tell who might wear each hat on the list. For example: helmet—football player, hard hat—construction worker, baseball cap—baseball player.

4 Begin by asking children if the monkeys in *Caps for Sale* were real or make believe. Then, read *Curious George* by H. A. Rey. After completing the story, have children tell about all the things Curious George did that real monkeys could not do (e.g., he talks, he goes to jail, etc.). Write their ideas on the chalkboard. Next, read a factual account of monkeys from a science book or encyclopedia. Again, ask children to tell you what they learned about monkeys from this reading and write out their suggestions. Then, give each child a sheet of 8 1/2" x 11" paper. Have them fold it in half and label one side "Real" and the other "Make-Believe." Have them draw something a real monkey could do on one side and something a make-believe monkey could do on the other. When complete, ask them to tell what they have drawn.

5 Students can create their own monkeys. Give each of them two brown or tan pom-pons, two eyes, one small piece of black yarn, a brown pipe cleaner, and a 5" x 8" index card. Students should glue down the two pom-pons, one on top of the other, for the monkey. Use the piece of black yarn to create a mouth. Then, curl the pipe cleaner and glue it down next to the body. Finally, draw a cap and glue it on top of his head. Draw arms and legs and glue them onto the body. Decorate the room with the monkeys.

An Extra Treat

Since monkeys like to eat peanuts and bananas, this might be an especially enjoyable time to have the students prepare peanut butter and banana sandwiches. You will need to buy enough bananas so that each child will have a half. You will also need a jar of peanut butter and a knife. Have students cut the bananas in half. Cut them in half again, lengthwise this time, and spread one half with peanut butter. Place the other half of the banana section on top to complete the sandwich.

From *Read It Again! More Book 1*, published by Good Year Books. Copyright © 1991 Terri Christman and Liz Rothlein.

CLOUDY WITH A CHANCE OF MEATBALLS

Author
Judi Barrett

Illustrator
Ron Barrett

Publisher
Atheneum, 1981

Pages	**Grade Level**
30	2-3

Additional Books by Barrett
Animals Should Definitely Not Act Like People; Animals Should Definitely Not Wear Clothing; Benjamin's 365 Birthdays; Snake Is Totally Tail

Summary
While Grandpa cooks breakfast, he accidentally flips a pancake onto his grandson Henry's head. This incident triggers the bedtime story Grandpa later tells to his granddaughter and Henry. It is a make-believe story about the town of Chewandswallow. This town was like small towns everywhere except that there were no food stores. The people living there got their food from the sky three times a day: breakfast, lunch and dinner. All went smoothly until the day when the weather took a turn for the worse. So much food came down in such unusual combinations that the people had to move away.

Introduction
Have you ever heard the expression "It's raining cats and dogs!" What do you think it means? The story we are about to hear is titled *Cloudy with a Chance of Meatballs*. Can anyone guess what the title means? Can you get any clues by looking at the cover? (Show the cover or, if it has been removed, show children the two-page spread showing hamburgers falling from the sky.) Once children have had an opportunity to predict, proceed with the story.

Key Vocabulary
After you read the story, write the following words on the chalkboard and choral read:

breakfast	story	town	weather
food	sky	meal	pancake

Key Vocabulary Instruction
Give each student eight 3" x 5" index cards. Have children write one vocabulary word on each card and pronounce the words to themselves. Next, have them illustrate the word on the back of each card. Ask them to place their cards in ABC order.

CLOUDY WITH A CHANCE OF MEATBALLS

Discussion Questions

1 Where did Grandpa get his idea for this story? (While cooking breakfast, he flipped a pancake onto Henry's head.)

2 Would you like to live in the town of Chewandswallow? Why or why not? (Answers may vary.)

3 What are the advantages and disadvantages of living in the town of Chewandswallow where the food falls from the sky? (Answers may vary.)

4 In this story, you heard about and saw the many different foods that fell from the sky. What food/foods would you like to have fall from the sky? (Answers may vary.)

5 What did the Sanitation Department do with the food that fell on the houses, sidewalks, and lawns? (Cleaned it up and fed it to the dogs and cats; emptied it into the oceans for the fish, turtles and whales; and put it back into the earth to make the soil richer.)

6 What did you think was the most interesting thing that happened in the town of Chewandswallow? (Answers may vary.)

7 The people leave the town of Chewandswallow. Would you have left? Explain. (Answers may vary.)

8 At the end of the story, Henry and his sister think the snow and sun look like mashed potatoes with a pat of butter. What other things have you seen that look like food? (Answers may vary.)

Bulletin Board

Label the bulletin board with *Cloudy with a Chance of Meatballs,* using white lettering. The background should be blue. Cut out large clouds from white construction paper and place them up near the title to represent the sky. Ask the students to cut out pictures of foods from magazines that they would like to see fall from the sky; the pictures could also be of foods that actually fell from the sky in the town of Chewandswallow. Adhere the pictures of the food to the bulletin board as if it was falling from the sky.

From *Read It Again! More Book 1*, published by Good Year Books. Copyright © 1991 Terri Christman and Liz Rothlein.

CLOUDY
WITH A
CHANCE OF
MEATBALLS

Name_____ Date_____

**ACTIVITY
SHEET 1**

Directions
Here are breakfast, lunch and dinner plates. Draw what you
would like to fall from the sky for each meal.

BREAKFAST

LUNCH

DINNER

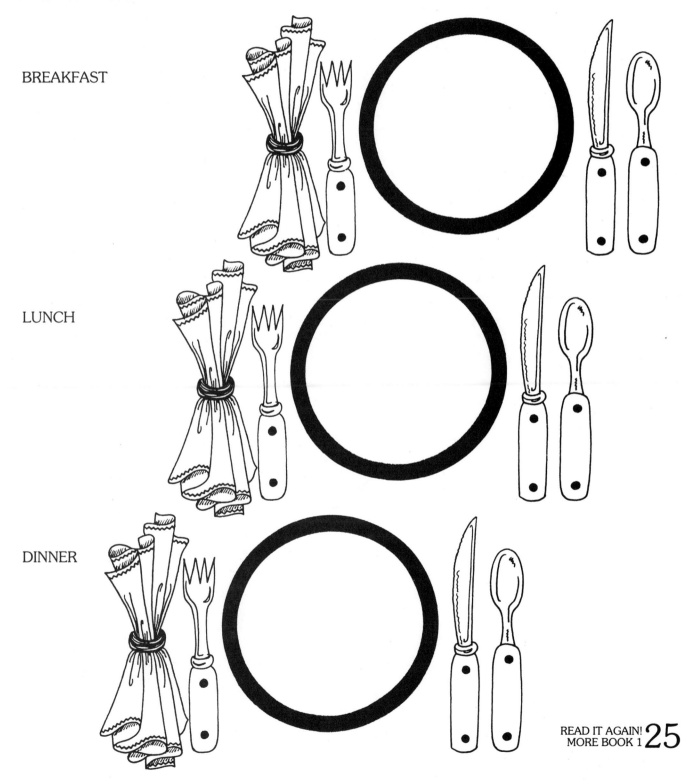

Name_____ Date_____

Directions

There are many compound words in *Cloudy with a Chance of Meatballs*. A compound word is one word that is made when two words are put together. Read the two words on these meatballs. Put the two words together on the lines below each meatball. You have made a compound word.

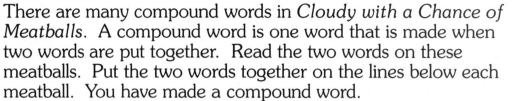

bed time	every where	what ever
_____	_____	_____

down stairs	school house	towns people
_____	_____	_____

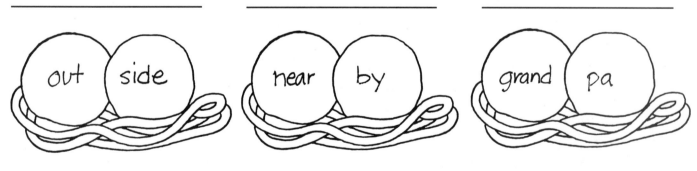

out side	near by	grand pa
_____	_____	_____

Name_____ Date_____

**ACTIVITY
SHEET 3**

Directions
Below are three weather reports from *Cloudy with a Chance of Meatballs*. Read each one and illustrate what it looked like in the town of Chewandswallow. In the last box, create your own weather report for your town/city.

1. After a brief shower of orange juice, low clouds of sunnyside eggs moved in followed by pieces of toast. Butter and jelly sprinkled down for the toast.

2. Frankfurters blew in the northwest at about five miles an hour. There were mustard clouds nearby. Then the wind shifted to the east and brought in baked beans. A drizzle of soda finished off the meal.

3. Lambchops becoming heavy at times with occasional ketchup. Periods of peas and baked potatoes were followed by a gradual clearing, with a wonderful gelatin setting in the west.

4. _____

_____

CLOUDY WITH A CHANCE OF MEATBALLS

Additional Activities

1 Each student will need a sheet of black construction paper, a sheet of white construction paper, several cotton balls, glue, scissors, and crayons. Have the students first glue their cotton balls to the sheet of black construction paper to form clouds. Then have them draw and color their favorite foods on the white construction paper. Cut out the drawings and glue them below the cotton clouds. Their food will be falling out of the sky, just like in Chewandswallow.

2 The students listened to many food weather reports throughout this story. This would be an ideal time to invite a meteorologist who does weather reports on the radio or television into your classroom. Have your students prepare questions in advance.

3 Help children study the weather closely over the course of a month. Each day select a student to cut out the weather report from the newspaper or write down a report heard on radio or television. Have the student tell the class about the report. (If possible, have students give the report daily over the school's speaker system for all classes to hear.) Attach the reports to the monthly calendar. At the end of the month, create a graph showing how many days it rained, how many days it was above a given temperature, how many inches of snow there were, etc.

4 The people from Chewandswallow solved their problem by leaving town. Have students think about other ways they could have solved their problem. List these solutions on the chalkboard and choral read them. Then have each student choose one of the possibilities and tell more about it in paragraph form (a group story is an alternative). Ask children to illustrate their work and share their new endings with the class.

5 As a class, list all the places to buy food in your neighborhood—everything from groceries to restaurants. Then have the students decide whether they would rather live in Chewandswallow, a place with no food stores, or their own town/city that has food stores. Have them defend their choice in paragraph form.

An Extra Treat

As a class, prepare one of the foods seen in *Cloudy with a Chance of Meatballs.* For example, you may want to bring in an electric skillet, oil, pancake mix, and pancake syrup and have the students create their own pancakes. Or, you could bring in a box of instant mashed potatoes. The students could then make their own mashed potatoes in individual bowls or cups.

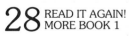

From *Read It Again! More Book 1*, published by Good Year Books. Copyright © 1991 Terri Christman and Liz Rothlein.

CROW BOY

Author
Taro Yashima

Illustrator
Taro Yashima

Publisher
The Viking Press, 1955

Pages	Grade Level
35	K-3

Other Books by Yashima
*Umbrella; Youngest One;
Seashore Story*

Summary
Chibi is a shy and lonely boy who has been treated badly by his classmates throughout five years of school. It isn't until Mr. Isobe, his sixth-grade teacher, recognizes his many talents that he is able to gain the respect he deserves.

Introduction
This is a story about a shy little boy named Chibi who, for five years of school, was mistreated by the other children. The children would not play with him; they made faces at him and were mean to him. Why do you think they were so unkind to him? How do you think Chibi felt? What do you think will happen to Chibi in this story?

Key Vocabulary Words
Write the following words on the chalkboard and choral read them:

tiny	school	crow	voices
nicknamed	imitate	lonely	village

Key Vocabulary Instruction
Place each vocabulary word on an index card. Make as many cards as you need so that each student will have a card with one vocabulary word on it. Divide the students into two teams. Pronounce a word from the list. Have any student who thinks he/she has the word jump up and pronounce it. The first student who identifies the word correctly gets a point for the team. The game continues until each word is repeated several times.

CROW BOY

Discussion Questions

1 What does it mean in the story where it says "Chibi found many ways to kill time?" (Answers may vary.)

2 What were some of the things that Chibi did on the playground? (Answers may vary but might include: listened for different sounds, watched insects.)

3 What did the teacher, Mr. Isobe, like about Chibi? (Answers may vary but might include: his black and white drawings, his handwriting, etc.)

4 Chibi was the only one in the class that had perfect attendance after six years of school. Why do you think Chibi continued to come to school every day even though he had no friends and wasn't treated very well? (Answers may vary.)

5 Why do you think Chibi was so shy? (Answers may vary.)

6 At the end of the story it said, "Chibi stretched his growing shoulders proudly like a grown-up man." Why do you think this happened? (Answers may vary.)

7 Chibi and Crow Boy were both nicknames. How did he get both of these names? (Chibi meant tiny boy, which he was; Crow Boy, because he understood crows so well.)

8 Why do you think the other children called him stupid and slow-poke? (Answers may vary.)

Bulletin Board

Put the caption "The Thing I Do Best" on the bulletin board. Using the award pattern provided, ask each student to complete a badge by either naming or illustrating one of his/her accomplishments that other people may not know about. (Some children may need some encouragement in identifying something they do well.) Adhere the completed awards to the bulletin board.

As an alternative to this activity, have children create awards for the characters they have read or heard about in other books.

From *Read It Again! More Book 1*, published by Good Year Books. Copyright © 1991 Terri Christman and Liz Rothlein.

CROW
BOY

Name _____ Date _____

ACTIVITY
SHEET 1

Directions

Use the picture to hunt for each of the following:

1. Find all the  (crows) and circle them. I found _____ crows.

2. Find all the (leaves) and color them green. I found _____ leaves.

3. Find all the (flowers) and color them red. I found _____ flowers.

4. Find all the (insects) and color them brown. I found _____ insects.

CROW
BOY

Directions
Crow Boy walked back and forth to school on the same route each day. Starting at Crow Boy's house, help him find his way to school by drawing a line on the best path. (Hint: Try out your ideas by tracing the routes with your finger before you use your pencil or crayon.)

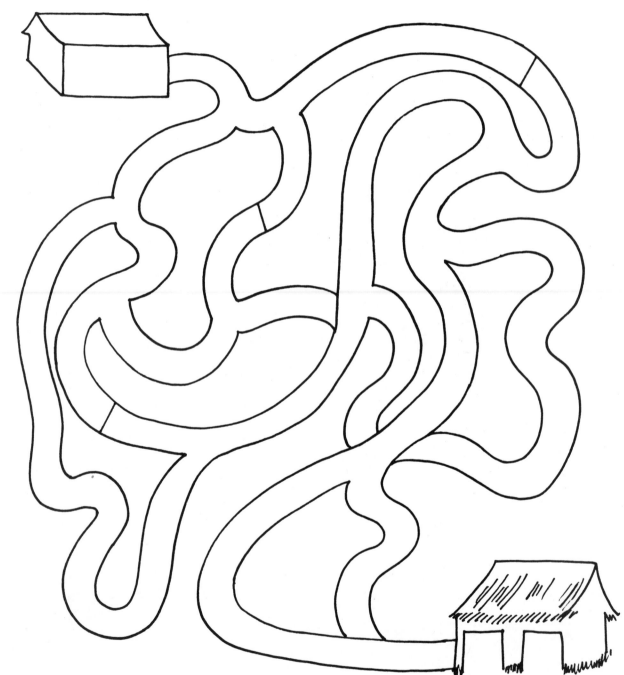

Name_____ Date_____

From *Read It Again! More Book 1*, published by Good Year Books. Copyright © 1991 Terri Christman and Liz Rothlein.

**ACTIVITY
SHEET 3**

Directions

Imagine that the people of the village have not seen Chibi in several days. Make a missing person poster that they could use to help find him.

Have you seen Chibi?

Name: _____

Address: _____

Height: _____

Weight: _____

Color of hair: _____

Color of eyes: _____

Clothing: _____

Special features: _____

_____

Last seen: _____

_____

If you have seen him call: _____

CROW BOY

Additional Activities

1 Chibi was not accepted by the other school children and he was lonely. Read other stories in which the main character is an outsider, e.g., Hans Christian Andersen's *The Ugly Duckling*. How are the characters alike? How are they different? Do you think both stories ended happily? Why or why not?

2 Read the dedication in the beginning of *Crow Boy* to the students. Discuss what a dedication to a book signifies. Ask students to think about what dedication they might write if they authored a book. If students are writing books of their own, incorporate the idea of writing dedications for the books.

3 In this story, Crow Boy imitated the sounds of different crows (baby crow, mother crow, father crow, etc.). Ask the students to each think of an animal he/she would like to imitate. Allow time for them to imitate the sounds as others guess the animal. Encourage them to try out different sounds, just as Chibi did.

4 If possible, invite someone into the class who speaks and writes Japanese. Before the guest arrives, help children to think of some questions they would like to ask. As an alternative, bring in some library books with Japanese characters for the class to examine. After everyone has had ample time to look at the characters, give students paintbrushes and black paint so they can experiment in drawing characters of their own.

An Extra Treat

Every day Chibi carried the same lunch to school. It was a rice ball wrapped in a radish leaf. Rice is one of the most popular foods in Japan where Crow Boy lived. Try making your own rice balls by following this recipe.

> 2 cups cooked rice
> 1 cup grated carrots
> 1/4 cup rice syrup
>   (available in oriental markets
>   and health food stores)

Mix all the ingredients together in a pan. Heat the mixture until it thickens. Form the mixture into balls.

Japanese people eat their food with eating utensils called chopsticks. Show the students how to hold chopsticks. Allow them to practice using chopsticks by picking up popcorn, potato chips, bits of cheese, etc.

From *Read It Again! More Book 1*, published by Good Year Books. Copyright © 1991 Terri Christman and Liz Rothlein.

DANNY AND THE DINOSAUR

Author
Syd Hoff

Illustrator
Syd Hoff

Publisher
Harper & Row, Publishers, 1958

Pages	Grade Level
64	K-3

Other Books by Hoff
Sammy the Seal; Julius; Oliver; Chester; Little Chief; Stanley; Grizzwold; Who Will Be My Friends?; Albert the Albatross

Summary
One of the dinosaurs Danny visits in the museum comes to life and the two go out to play together. They play hide and seek, Danny rides on the dinosaur's tail and watches a ball game from his back, and they go to the zoo. After a fun-filled day, the two friends part; the dinosaur returns to the museum and Danny goes home.

Introduction
Show children the cover of the book and tell them that the story they will hear is all about the things Danny and the dinosaur do together. Ask: What are some of the things they might do together? Where will they go? Will the people they meet be afraid of the dinosaur? What do you think you would do if you saw a dinosaur who could walk and talk? After reading, compare their predictions with the story.

Key Vocabulary
Write the following words on the chalkboard and choral read them:

dinosaurs	hippos	monkeys	lions
giraffes	seals	elephants	bears

Key Vocabulary Instruction
Give each student a plain sheet of white paper (8 1/2" x 11"). Ask students to fold the piece of paper in half lengthwise once and then again. Next, fold the paper in half the other way, once and then again. Now, open the sheet of paper; there should be eight squares. Ask the students to write one vocabulary word in each box. Talk about what each of the animals looks like and share pictures of them with the children. Next, have children draw a picture to represent each word. Finally, using the sheet of paper with the vocabulary words as a bingo card and pieces of corn or chips, play bingo by calling out the vocabulary words.

DANNY AND THE DINOSAUR

Discussion Questions

1 Where did Danny meet his friend the dinosaur? (At the museum.)

2 What other things, besides the dinosaur, did Danny see at the zoo? (Indians, bears, Eskimos, guns, and swords.)

3 What did the dinosaur mean when he said, "It's good to take an hour or two off after a hundred million years?" (Answers may vary.)

4 Why do you think the policeman stared and dogs barked at the dinosaur? (Answers may vary.)

5 Which of the things Danny and the dinosaur did together do you think would have been the most fun? Why? (Answers may vary.)

6 Why wouldn't Danny allow the dinosaur to eat the grass? (There was a sign that said, "PLEASE KEEP OFF.")

7 Where do you think would be a good place for a dinosaur to hide? (Answers may vary.)

8 How do you think Danny felt when he said goodbye to the dinosaur? Explain. (Answers may vary.)

Bulletin Board

Label the bulletin board "Our Dinosaur Pets." Use the children's creations from Activity Sheet 2 to design a bulletin board.

Special Notes about the Activities

Activity 2: Take the class to the library and have children find books picturing dinosaurs. Have them use these books as they create their own dinosaurs on the worksheet with crayons, construction paper, etc.

Activity 3: After reading the story, recall the places that Danny and the dinosaur went together. List them in order on the chalkboard. Tell children that they are going to make a map of the places Danny and the dinosaur visited. Give them the Activity 3 worksheet and discuss. Show them how to use the list on the board to help them. (The map has been started for them.)

From *Read It Again! More Book 1*, published by Good Year Books. Copyright © 1991 Terri Christman and Liz Rothlein.

DANNY AND THE DINOSAUR

Name_____ Date_____

Directions

Pretend that you could have a dinosaur for a pet. Draw or write about four things you and your dinosaur would do together.

Name_____ Date_____

Directions
Tell about your dinosaur friend.

_____ and the Dinosaur

Dinosaur's name _____

Dinosaur's address _____

Height _____

Weight _____

What does he look like?_____

_____

What are his favorite foods?_____

_____

What does he like to do? _____

_____

From *Read It Again! More Book 1*, published by Good Year Books. Copyright © 1991 Terri Christman and Liz Rothlein.

Name_____ Date_____

Directions
Use the dinosaur parts below to create imaginary dinosaurs.
Connect a head, with a body and feet. After you have created
your imaginary dinosaurs, paste the parts together. Select
one of these dinosaurs and pretend it is your pet. Next, paste
your pet dinosaur on a sheet of paper and write a short story
about it.

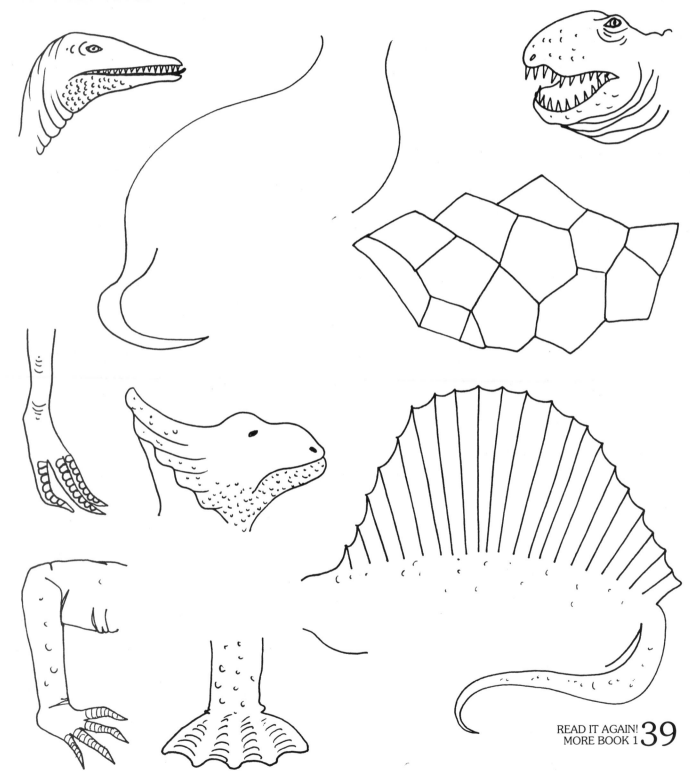

DANNY AND THE DINOSAUR

Additional Activities

1 Obtain copies of the books *If the Dinosaurs Came Back* by Bernard Most and *The Secret Dinosaur* by Marilyn Hirsh. *If the Dinosaurs Came Back* is an imaginative fantasy about a boy who dreams he has a dinosaur of his own. The boy dreams about all the things the dinosaur could do from pushing rain clouds away to getting kites from trees. *The Secret Dinosaur* is a fantasy about two children and the ways they try to hide a hungry dinosaur. Compare and contrast these books with *Danny and the Dinosaur.* How are the dinosaurs alike? Different? Are the children in the stories ever afraid of the dinosaurs? Are the other people in the story fearful when they meet the dinosaur? What happens to the dinosaurs at the end of each story?

2 Have the students pretend that it is possible to bring back the dinosaurs. However, to do this they must convince their parents and neighbors that it would be a good idea. Divide the children into pairs or small groups and ask them to create a poster or flyer which would convince people that dinosaurs should be a part of the community. Encourage the children to think of all the things Danny's dinosaur could do. Ask them to think of other ways that dinosaurs could be helpful. Allow time for children to share these posters with each other as well as with other classes.

3 Have the children conduct an interview with family, friends and neighbors about the kinds of things they would like a dinosaur to do for them if they had one. Ask each student to compile a list of all the responses they get. After all interviews are completed, as a class project, compile the data. If feasible, graph the responses.

4 There are many excellent informational books about dinosaurs such as *Dinosaurs* by Kathleen Daly or *Now You Can Read About Dinosaurs* by Harry Stanton. Share some of these books with the children. Once they become familiar with information about dinosaurs—when they lived, their habitats, food, size, etc.—discuss the problems a dinosaur would have if it lived near your school. What problems might the dinosaur cause the neighbors? The school children and teachers?

5 Provide the children with large brown grocery bags. Ask them to create a paper bag puppet which represents a dinosaur. Allow time for the children to role play being a dinosaur.

An Extra Treat

For snack time, allow students to make their own dinosaur creatures from an assortment of vegetables. Provide them with toothpicks, paper towels, and a variety of vegetables such as celery, brussel sprouts, broccoli, pea pods, carrots, cauliflower, radishes, mushrooms, and lettuce. Have them place the vegetables on the toothpicks and arrange them on the towel to form dinosaurs.

From *Read It Again! More Book 1*, published by Good Year Books. Copyright © 1991 Terri Christman and Liz Rothlein.

THE FIVE CHINESE BROTHERS

Author
Claire Huchet Bishop

Illustrator
Kurt Wise

Publisher
Coward-McCann, Inc., 1938

Pages	Grade Level
46	K-3

Other Books by Bishop
Lafayette: French American Hero; Man Who Lost his Head; Martin de Porres, Hero; Mozart: Music Magician; Twenty-two Bears; Twenty and Ten: As Told by Janet Joly

Summary
Once there were five Chinese brothers. Although they looked alike, there was something special about each one. The first could swallow the sea, the second had an iron neck, the third could stretch and stretch his legs, the fourth could not be burned, and the fifth could hold his breath indefinitely. When the first brother gets into trouble, all of the brothers use their abilities to help. They are successful and live happily ever after.

Introduction
Have you ever heard a story about a person who could do something that couldn't really happen? Tell us about the story and the person. Why was s/he a make-believe person? (If ideas are not forthcoming, help children recall stories of make-believe that you have read together; you may want to add characters such as Superman.) Have you ever read a story about make-believe animals? What were they? (Recall stories such as *Petunia, Alexander and the Wind-up Mouse,* and *Danny and the Dinosaur* from this book as well as others you have read.) Continue to help children see the distinction between real and make-believe by pointing to examples from stories they know. When the concept is clearly grasped, introduce this story by telling children that they are going to hear a story about five Chinese brothers, each one with a very special ability. Add that the story is a tale that was first told in China many, many years ago. Ask them to listen carefully so that after they have heard the story you can talk together about the make-believe people they hear about.

Key Vocabulary
Write the following words on the board and choral read them:

Chinese	brothers	fourth	sea
fifth	first	second	third

Key Vocabulary Instruction
Using the pattern below, cut out eight fish from construction paper. Write one of the vocabulary words on each of the fish and tape them to the chalkboard. Draw a large circle on the chalkboard to represent the sea. Ask students to select one of the "fish words," pronounce it, and use it in a sentence. If done correctly, the student tapes the fish inside the sea. This activity continues until all the fish are in the sea.

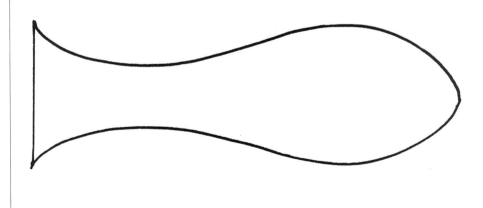

THE FIVE CHINESE BROTHERS

Discussion Questions

1 Do you think this story could really happen? What parts were make-believe? (Answers may vary.)

2 What do you think happened to the boy that went fishing with the First Chinese Brother? (Answers may vary, but he probably drowned.)

3 What unusual or make-believe abilities did each of the Five Chinese Brothers possess or have?

First Chinese Brother	(swallowed the sea)
Second Chinese Brother	(had an iron neck)
Third Chinese Brother	(stretched and stretched his legs)
Fourth Chinese Brother	(could not be burned)
Fifth Chinese Brother	(held his breath indefinitely)

4 How did the brothers trick the judge? (Answers may vary, but may include that they wanted to say goodbye to their brother and then they traded places with each other.)

5 Which of the Five Chinese Brothers would you most like to be? Why? (Answers may vary.)

6 Of all the things the Five Chinese Brothers did, which do you think was the smartest? (Answers may vary.)

7 Do you think the First Chinese Brother should have been punished because the boy who went fishing with him disappeared? Why or why not? (Answers may vary.)

8 What do you think would have happened if the judge had decided on a different punishment? (Answers may vary.)

Bulletin Board

Each brother in *The Five Chinese Brothers* had a characteristic that helped him in some way. Pretend there was a Sixth Chinese Brother. What characteristic do you think he might have? Ask children to create an illustration of the Sixth Chinese Brother and write at least one sentence describing his characteristic and how it could help him. Adhere the illustrations and descriptions to the bulletin board that is labeled, "The Sixth Chinese Brother."

Special Notes about the Activities

Activity 1: Tell children to look at the pictures in the boxes on the worksheet and decide which happened first, second, etc. Then cut out the words first, second, third, fourth, and fifth and paste them under the pictures in the order that they happened. After pasting, color the pictures, cut them apart, and put them in the correct order. Staple the pictures together to make a booklet. The first box is the cover.

From *Read It Again! More Book 1*, published by Good Year Books. Copyright © 1991 Terri Christman and Liz Rothlein.

Name_____ Date_____

**ACTIVITY
SHEET 1**

Directions
Put these pictures in order and make your own book.

| FIRST | SECOND | THIRD | FOURTH | FIFTH |

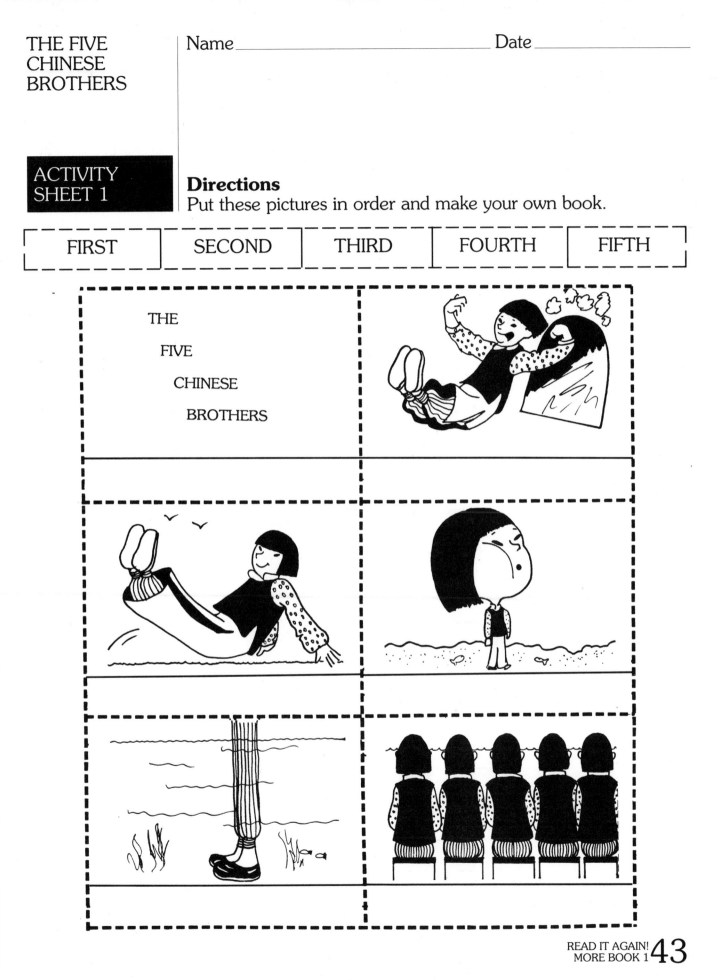

Name_____ Date_____

Directions
Select one of the Five Chinese Brothers and illustrate a different special or make-believe ability that he could have had. For example, if you pick the Second Chinese Brother, instead of an iron neck, give him arms that he could make as long as he wanted. Use this page to tell about his special ability.

Which brother did you select? _____

What special ability did he have? _____

Draw your picture of this brother in the box.

How could his special ability have helped him in the story? _____

_____

_____

From *Read It Again! More Book 1*, published by Good Year Books. Copyright © 1991 Terri Christman and Liz Rothlein.

THE FIVE
CHINESE
BROTHERS

Name_____ Date_____

Directions
In this story, some things were make-believe (things that couldn't really happen) and some things were real (things that could really happen). Read the following sentences. Put an M on the blank if it is make-believe and an R if it is real.

_____ 1. The First Chinese Brother took a little boy fishing.

_____ 2. The First Chinese Brother swallowed the sea.

_____ 3. The Five Chinese Brothers lived by the sea.

_____ 4. The First Chinese Brother went fishing and brought back fish to sell at the market.

_____ 5. The Second Chinese Brother had an iron neck.

_____ 6. The Third Chinese Brother could stretch and stretch his neck.

_____ 7. The Five Chinese Brothers tricked the judge by trading places with each other.

_____ 8. The Fourth Chinese Brother could not be burned.

_____ 9. The Fifth Chinese Brother could hold his breath forever.

_____ 10. The Five Chinese Brothers lived with their mother.

_____ 11. The Five Chinese Brothers all looked exactly alike.

_____ 12. The Five Chinese Brothers lived happily for many years.

Illustrate what you think was the most unbelievable or make-believe happening in the story.

THE FIVE CHINESE BROTHERS

Additional Activities

To help the students better understand the Chinese culture--their language, writing system, and customs—do some of the following activities:

1 The Chinese language is spoken in many ways throughout China; however, the Chinese language is written the same throughout the country. A few years ago, the National Republic of China declared Mandarin Chinese as the official language. Help students get a better understanding of what this language is like by teaching them to sing "Happy Birthday" in Chinese.

English words	Happy Birthday
Chinese words	Zuni Shenri
English sounds	zoo nee shen ree

English	Hap py Birth day to you
Chinese	Zu ni Shen ri Kuai le
English sounds	zoo nee shen ree kwa lee

2 Locate China on a map or globe. Then using an encyclopedia or books such as *Passport to China* by Stephen Keeler, share information about China's population, size, climate, vegetation, etc.

3 Bring an abacus. Tell children that this tool was created by the ancient Chinese and used by them to add, subtract, multiply, divide, and to calculate square and cube roots. Demonstrate how it could be used and provide time for children to experiment with it.

4 Obtain books such as *Chinese Writing—An Introduction* by Dianne Wolff, or *Chinese Calligraphy* by Chiang Yee, and allow the students to investigate the art of Chinese writing. Tell them that the Chinese do not have an alphabet for reading and writing like we do. Instead, they use characters (called *dz* in Chinese) to represent words or ideas. The following are examples of some Chinese characters that represent the English words indicated:

| one | two | three |

Have children try drawing some of the characters which you have reprinted on the chalkboard or overhead.

From *Read It Again! More Book 1*, published by Good Year Books. Copyright © 1991 Terri Christman and Liz Rothlein.

THE FIVE
CHINESE
BROTHERS

5 Introduce the students to the tangram puzzle that has seven pieces which was developed by the Chinese. The Chinese used the tangram puzzle pieces to make pictures of fish, birds, houses, etc. Ask children to trace the pattern pieces below on tagboard and cut them out. (Have pattern pieces prepared for younger children.) Then, allow time for each student to create a design using the tangram puzzle pieces. Share these designs.

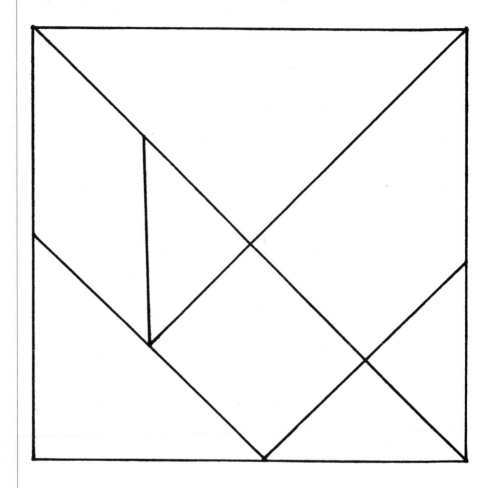

THE LITTLE HOUSE

Author
Virginia Lee Burton

Illustrator
Virginia Lee Burton

Publisher
Houghton Mifflin Company, 1942

Pages	Grade Level
40	Preschool-3

Other Books by Burton
Katy and the Big Snow; Mike Mulligan and his Steam Shovel

Summary
A once charming country house is anxious and lonely as a city is built around it. The Little House misses the daisies, apple trees, birds and all the changes of the seasons that it saw in the country. Finally, the great-great granddaughter of the first owner moves the Little House back to the country and it is happy again.

Introduction
This is a story about a little house who loved living in the country. Eventually, highways and skyscrapers surrounded the house and the countryside disappeared. Let's think together about all the things that might surround a little house in the middle of the city. (List children's ideas on the chalkboard.) Now, let's make a list of all the things that might be around the house in the country. After we finish the book, we can compare our lists with what we found out in the story.

Key Vocabulary
After children have heard the story, write the following words on the chalkboard and choral read:

countryside	fall	spring	seasons
summer	city	house	winter

Key Vocabulary Instruction
Draw a house on the chalkboard. Be sure the house has a chimney, roof, door, two windows, two trees, and a sidewalk. Place one vocabulary word on each item. Read each sentence below and call on a student to pronounce the vocabulary word that completes the sentence. If they are correct, have them come up to the chalkboard and color in (using colored chalk) that part of the picture that has the word in it. When they are all finished, the picture will be colored.

1. The Little House lived in the _____. (countryside)

2. In the _____ the days grew longer and the Little House watched for buds on the trees. (spring)

3. Way off in the distance at night, the Little House could see the lights of the _____. (city)

4. In the _____ she watched children swimming in the pool. (summer)

5. In the _____ she watched the children go back to school. (fall)

6. The four _____ are fall, winter, spring, and summer. (seasons)

7. The Little _____ watched them make roads. (House)

8. In the _____ she saw the countryside covered in snow. (winter)

THE LITTLE HOUSE

From *Read It Again! More Book 1*, published by Good Year Books.   Copyright © 1991 Terri Christman and Liz Rothlein.

Discussion Questions

1 What did the Little House like about living in the country? (Answers may vary but might include: it was peaceful; quiet; could see the moon, stars, and sun.)

2 Why do you think the Little House was curious about the city? (Answers may vary.)

3 What didn't the Little House like about living in the city? (Answers may vary but might include: it was too noisy; dusty; crowded; couldn't see the moon, stars, and sun like before, etc.)

4 Why do you think the children who grew up in the Little House moved to the city? (Answers may vary.)

5 What do you think would have happened to the Little House if the great-great granddaughter hadn't come along and moved it back to the country? (Answers may vary.)

6 Which season do you think the Little House liked best? (Answers may vary.)

7 Why could the Little House only see the sun at noon while it was in the city? (Because tall buildings blocked out the sun.)

8 What changes occurred in the countryside where the Little House was originally located? (Answers may vary but might include: horseless carriages were coming down the road, surveyors were surveying, a steam shovel dug a road through the hill, trucks dumped stones on the road.)

Bulletin Board

Divide the bulletin board in half. On one side, place the heading "Country Words" and on the other side place the heading "City Words." Pass out a 4" x 6" index card to each student. Have the students, using a crayon, write one word they heard in the story that would fit either on the "Country Words" side or the "City Words" side. Adhere these words under the correct headings. Once the bulletin board is complete, choral read the words each day the bulletin board is up. The students should be encouraged to add new words as they think of them.

Name_____   Date_____

Directions
Color and cut out the pictures below and paste them around
the correct tree (on next page) for each season.

From *Read It Again! More Book 1*, published by Good Year Books. Copyright © 1991 Terri Christman and Liz Rothlein.

FALL

WINTER

SPRING

SUMMER

THE
LITTLE
HOUSE

Name _____ Date _____

Directions
Pretend you could move your house or apartment where you live to another place. Draw a picture of where you would like to live and tell about it in the sentences below.

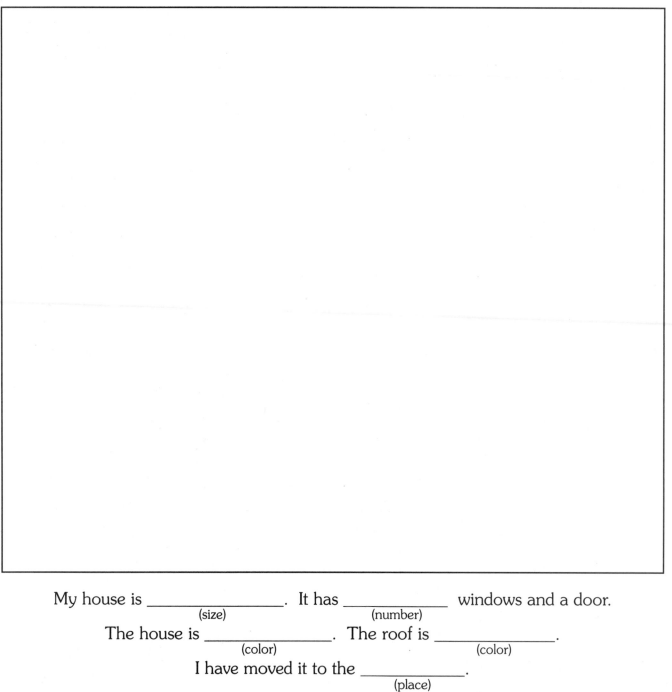

My house is _____. It has _____ windows and a door.
              (size)   (number)

The house is _____. The roof is _____.
         (color)   (color)

I have moved it to the _____.
            (place)

Name_____ Date_____

Directions
Read the phrases below that are taken from the book *The Little House*. These are all things the Little House watched. Draw a line from the phrase to the correct picture. Color the pictures.

1. watched the moon grow

2. watched big buildings going up

3. watched the trolley cars

4. watched the countryside around her

5. watched the city lights

6. watched them make a road

List other things the Little House watched. _____

_____

_____

THE LITTLE HOUSE

Additional Activities

1 One of the illustrations in *The Little House* shows a calendar indicating the different phases of the moon. As a class, chart the phases of the moon for several months so students can see how the moon repeats its cycle. This can be done by assigning a student a day to look for the moon and to draw how it appears on the calendar. Students can also check local newspapers for dates of full moon, half moon, etc.

2 Ask students to discuss any changes that may have occurred in their neighborhoods, such as new houses, roads, businesses being built, and so forth. Talk about the advantages and disadvantages of these changes. Invite older residents, grandparents, senior citizens, etc., who have lived in the neighborhood for years to speak to the class about changes they have observed. Share pictures, if possible.

3 On one piece of white poster board write "Country Life." On another piece of white poster board write "City Life." Give the students old magazines to cut pictures of things found in the city and things found in the country. Glue the pictures on the posterboard. The pictures can later be combined into a class collage or mural.

4 Ask student to bring in a shoe box to use in making their own Little House. Encourage them to make windows, doors, a chimney and other house features they can think of. Provide wallpaper and construction paper scraps, pieces of cloth, paint, etc. Display the Little Houses.

5 Tell the students that if they look closely at the Little House they will see a face. The windows are the eyes, the door is the nose, and the step is the mouth. Page through the book as children look for these features. Help them to observe how the face changes, first to sadness, then to happiness. Have the students design a house giving it facial features. Share the illustrations with classmates.

An Extra Treat

In this story, the Little House watched the apple trees burst into blossom in the spring. Then, in the summer, she watched the apples turn red and ripen. In the fall she watched the apples being picked. Bring in a bag of apples. Pull off any leaves and stems and wash the apples. Quarter ten apples and place them in a pot with 1/4 cup water. Boil the apples until they become very soft. Pour the cooked apples into a strainer that has a large bowl under it. Stir the mixture, allowing the applesauce to go through the strainer. Add sugar to taste. You and your students will enjoy homemade applesauce.

From *Read It Again! More Book 1*, published by Good Year Books. Copyright © 1991 Terri Christman and Liz Rothlein.

MADELINE

Author
Ludwig Bemelmans

Publisher
The Viking Press, 1939

Pages	**Grade Level**
44	Preschool-2

Other Books by Burton
Madeline and the Bad Hat;
Madeline and the Gypsies;
Madeline in London;
Madeline's Rescue;
Madeline's Christmas

Summary
This is one of a series of books written about a little girl named Madeline. Madeline lives in a house in Paris with eleven other girls and Miss Clavel. In this story, Madeline has an appendicitis attack and is hurried to the hospital. She is showered with so much attention there than the other little girls think they should have their appendixes out, too.

Introduction
Introduce *Madeline* by reading and showing the illustrations on the first twelve pages of the book, ending with the words, "the smallest one was Madeline." Since the location and the kind of school Madeline attends are likely to be unfamiliar to most children, begin by showing them where Paris is on a map or globe. Follow by helping them to compare how Madeline lives with the way they do. Ask children: What kind of home do you think Madeline lives in? Why are all the little girls dressed alike? Why do they walk in two straight lines? Once the setting is established, complete the story.

Key Vocabulary
Write the following words on the chalkboard and choral read them:

twelve	cried	hospital	flowers
straight	appendix	visitors	lines

Key Vocabulary Instruction
Using the flower pattern provide on the next page, cut out eight flowers from different colors of construction paper. Write a vocabulary word on each of the flowers. Line the vocabulary flowers along the chalkboard tray. Next, draw a vase or flower pot with eight stems extending from it. Tell students you are making a flower arrangement for Madeline. Ask one student to select a flower and pronounce the word on it; then select another student to use it in a sentence. When both steps have been successfully completed, have them tape the flower to the stem. Continue until all flowers have been put onto the stem.

MADELINE

Discussion Questions

1 Who was Miss Clavel? (Answers may vary but may include that she is the woman who took care of the girls.)

2 What happened to Madeline one night? (She had an appendicitis attack.) Do any of you know what an appendix is? (Explain if necessary.)

3 How did the little girls get to the place where Madeline was? (On a bus.)

4 What was the biggest surprise for the little girls when they went to visit Madeline? (The scar on her stomach.)

5 Why did all the girls want to have their appendix out after they had visited Madeline? (Because they all wanted to get candy, toys, flowers, etc.)

6 Why didn't Miss Clavel call the doctor when she found all the girls crying and wanting their appendixes out? (She knew they were not really sick.)

Bulletin Board
Put the following caption in big, bold letters on the bulletin board, "GET WELL MADELINE." Ask the students to find pictures in magazines, illustrate, or write a description of gift they would take to Madeline. Adhere the "gifts" to the bulletin board.

Special Notes about the Activities
Activity 3: Gather several telephone books for your area. Divide your class into small groups and give each group one of the books to work with. Show them how to locate the emergency, police, fire, and hospital telephone numbers (usually inside the front cover). Help them enter these numbers on the correct lines on the form. Help, too, as they enter in their own names and addresses and use school records to complete the rest of the form. Encourage them to keep this booklet at home in a place where they can always find it.

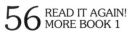
From *Read It Again! More Book 1*, published by Good Year Books. Copyright © 1991 Terri Christman and Liz Rothlein.

Name_____ Date_____

Directions

Madeline's story is told in rhyme. You can practice rhyming by filling in the blanks on the flowers with a rhyming word from the box. Color the flowers and cut them out. Glue them on a blank piece of paper. Draw a vase, stems, and leaves. You will have a beautiful vase of rhyming flowers.

bed	line	sad	by
light	ice	hours	door

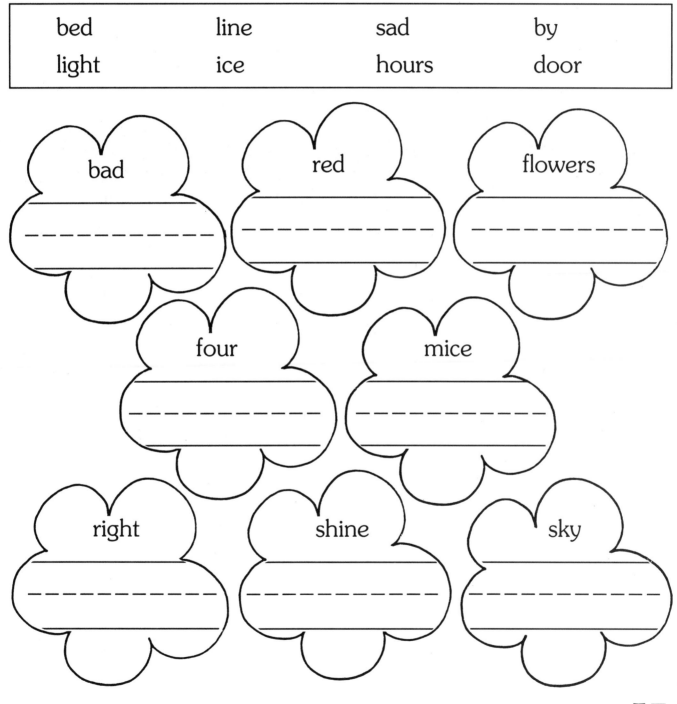

Name_____ Date_____

Directions
Read each of the sentences or phrases on the girls below.
Then read the phrases on the hats on the next page. Match
the hats with the girls, and paste the hats in place.

with some flowers
and a vase.

and the little girls
left in the rain.

Miss Clavel turned
on her light.

"Nurse," he said,
"it's an appendix!"

of sometimes looking
like a rabbit.

and went
to bed.

on her stomach
was a scar!

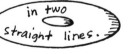
Madeline just said
"Pooh-pooh".

We want to have
our appendix out, too!

in two
straight lines.

MADELINE | Name_____ Date_____

Directions
Make your own telephone book and keep it in a safe place.

Name _____

Address _____

_____

If I need to, I can call _____

_____

_____

Emergency Number _____

Doctor _____

Hospital _____

Police _____

Fire _____

MADELINE

Additional Activities

1 Madeline's house was in Paris. Locate Paris on a map. Put the title of the book and the name of the author on an index card and tape it beside the world map. Stretch a piece of yarn from the index card to Paris. As you continue to read books to your students, put an index card up indicating the stories' settings, where the authors are from, etc. By the end of the year, your map will be surrounded by index cards. This is a great way to integrate social studies and literature.

2 Children can make their own bouquets for Madeline. Fold coffee filters in half once, then fold in half again. Provide small cups of red, blue, and yellow food coloring and cotton swabs. Instruct the children to dip the swab in the food color and then press it firmly onto the folded coffee filter. As the colors spread, the children will observe how new colors appear, e.g., green will appear when yellow and blue spread together. Allow the coffee filter to dry. Twist a pipe cleaner around the tip of the coffee filter. Open the filter and you have a flower for Madeline's bouquets.

3 Read the following books about going to the hospital: *The Operations* by Penny S. Anderson, *Why Am I Going to the Hospital?* by Claire Cilotta and Carole Livingston, *The Hospital Scares Me* by Paula Z. Hogan and Paul Hogan, and *Eric Needs Stitches* by Barbara Pavis Marino. Allow children to share their own experiences with hospitals. Invite a doctor and/or nurse into the classroom to discuss going to the hospital and what can be expected. Provide a question and answer period.

4 Give each student a sheet of white paper, 8 1/2" x 11". Next, ask them to fold it in half. They are now ready to make a get well card for Madeline, someone they know who is ill, or someone they know who might like to be cheered up. Don't forget to have them decorate their cards.

MAKE WAY FOR DUCKLINGS

Author
Robert McCloskey

Illustrator
Robert McCloskey

Pages	Grade Level
64	1-3

Other Books by McCloskey
*Lentil; Homer Price;
Centerburg Tales; Blueberries
for Sal; One Morning in Maine;
Time of Wonder; Burt Dow;
Deep Water Man*

Summary
Mr. and Mrs. Mallard are looking for a safe place to hatch and raise their ducklings. They want a place with no foxes in the woods and no turtles in the water. They find an island near the Public Garden for a quiet nesting spot. Once the ducklings are old enough, they move to the Public Garden with the help of Michael, the policeman.

Introduction
We are going to read a book about some mallard ducks. Robert McCloskey wrote the story and drew the illustrations. He tells us that he watched real ducklings for days to make his drawings better. Let's look at some of the pictures inside the book. Do you think these ducks look real? Why or why not? (Answers may vary.) Many of the buildings and the park you see in the illustrations can be found in the city of Boston, a city in the state of Massachusetts. Mr. McCloskey got many of the ideas for these drawings from the city that he knew so well. (Turn to the pages showing the State House, the Public Garden, and Louisburg Square as examples.) Proceed with reading the book.

Key Vocabulary
Write the following words on the chalkboard and choral read them:

ducklings	mallard	hatch	flew
swan	policeman	nest	island

Key Vocabulary Instruction
Provide each student with a sheet of 11" x 14" white paper as well as a copy of the eight eggs on page 64. Have them begin by drawing a nest that is big enough for all the eggs to fit in. Then, ask them to write one of the vocabulary words on each egg. As they practice reading the words to themselves, they can cut out the eggs and glue them in the nest. Children may want to color the eggs and the nest.

From *Read It Again! More Book 1*, published by Good Year Books. Copyright © 1991 Terri Christman and Liz Rothlein.

MAKE WAY FOR DUCKLINGS

Discussion Questions

1 Why were Mr. and Mrs. Mallard so careful about selecting a place to live? (Answers may vary.)

2 What did Mrs. Mallard like and dislike about the pond in the Public Garden? (She liked the peanuts the people fed her, but she didn't like the bicycle.)

3 Describe how Mrs. Mallard took care of her eggs. (Answers may vary.)

4 Mrs. Mallard taught her ducklings many things. What were they? What are some things your parents have taught you? (Answers may vary.)

5 How did Michael, the police officer, help Mrs. Mallard? (He fed her peanuts and helped her move her family safely across the street.)

6 What did you learn about ducks? (Answers may vary.)

7 How was the Mallard family like a human family? (Answers may vary.)

8 The ducklings' names were Jack, Kack, Lack, Mack, Nack, Ouack, Pack, and Quack. If the Mallards had more ducklings, what do you think they would name them? (Answers may vary.)

Bulletin Board

Give each student a copy of the mallard duck on page 65. Have them color it. Next, have them glue feathers, which they have colored and/or cut from drawing or construction paper, onto the wings. Have the students complete the sentence: If I were a duck I would like to live _____. Finally, display these on the bulletin board and label it "Make Way For Ducklings."

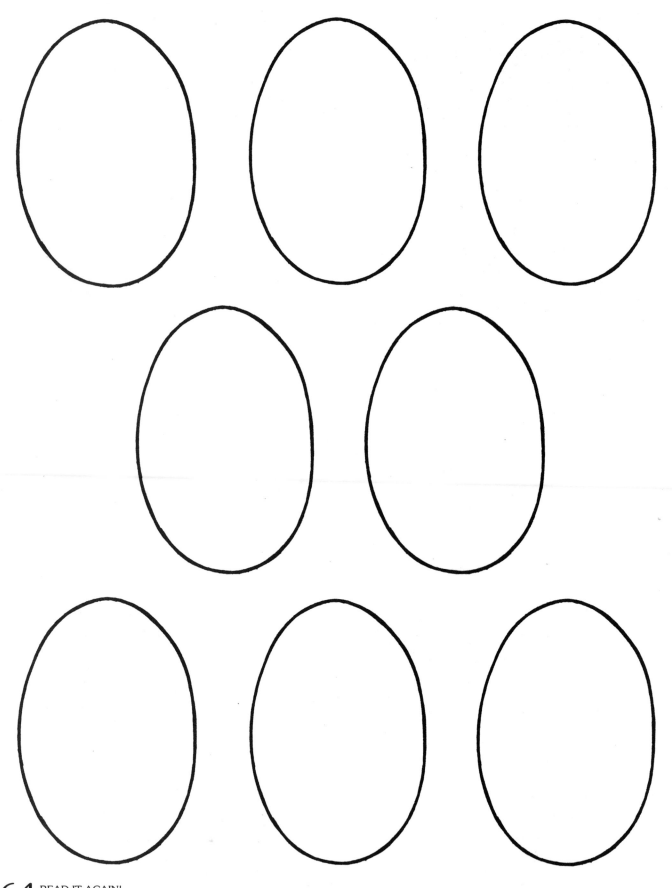

From *Read It Again! More Book 1*, published by Good Year Books. Copyright © 1991 Terri Christman and Liz Rothlein.

Name_____ Date_____

If I were a duck I would like to live _____

_____

_ _

_____

_____

_ _

_____

Name_____ Date _____

Directions
Draw pictures to show what the ducklings learned from Mrs. Mallard. Draw pictures to show what you have learned from a grown-up.

Mrs. Mallard taught her ducklings to

My _____ has taught me how to

From *Read It Again! More Book 1*, published by Good Year Books. Copyright © 1991 Terri Christman and Liz Rothlein.

Name _____ Date _____

Directions
Mrs. Mallard had eight ducklings. All of their names ended with <u>ack</u>. Pretend you were asked to think of names for some ducks. Using the word families provided, fill in the blanks with names.

ack   ed

Jack   _____

Kack   _____

Lack   _____

Mack   _____

Nack   _____

Ouack   _____

Pack   _____

Quack   _____

all   ell

_____   _____

_____   _____

_____   _____

_____   _____

_____   _____

_____   _____

_____   _____

_____   _____

Which name do you like best? _____

Turn the paper over and draw a duckling to go with the name you like best.

Name _____ Date _____

Directions

These pictures are from *Make Way for Ducklings*. Cut them out and put them back in order. Staple them together and color the pictures. You now have your own *Make Way for Ducklings* book.

Mr. and Mrs. Mallard were looking for a place to live.

The ducklings hatched.

Michael helped Mrs. Mallard and her ducklings cross the street.

They thought they had found a place to raise their babies until a boy on a bicycle rushed by.

The Mallards lived happily on the island.

Mrs. Mallard laid eight eggs.

They built a nest in some bushes near the water.

Mrs. Mallard taught her ducklings how to swim, dive, walk in a straight line, and keep away from things with wheels.

From *Read It Again! More Book 1*, published by Good Year Books. Copyright © 1991 Terri Christman and Liz Rothlein.

MAKE WAY FOR DUCKLINGS

Additional Activities

1 Invite a police officer into the classroom. Have the officer discuss why s/he wanted to become a police officer, how s/he became one, and what his/her duties are. Prepare students for the visit by talking with them about some of the questions they can ask the officer.

2 Have the students create dioramas of the Mallards' new home in the park. They can use a box (shoe boxes work especially well) and various materials such as leaves, branches, grass, feathers, etc. If they like, they can add Mrs. Mallard and the eight ducklings.

3 Our story ends with the Mallard family living happily on the island. Let's think of another adventure for one of the ducklings. Which one should we choose? What happens to him (her) when he (she) gets bigger? Prompt responses with questions such as: Do you think s/he might have gone for a swim alone? Where did s/he go? Who did s/he meet? How did s/he get home? Write out the children's ideas as they are offered. When the story is complete, read it together. You can extend the activity by having children write their own stories about one of the ducks.

4 Robert McCloskey includes many references to Boston, Massachusetts, in his story: Beacon Hill, the State House, the Charles River, Louisburg Square, etc. Ask children to work together or independently and write a paragraph describing what Mr. and Mrs. Mallard would see if they flew into their city or town. Ask them to add illustrations to their paragraphs and provide time for them to share their work.

An Extra Treat

Michael and other people throughout the story fed Mr. and Mrs. Mallard and their family peanuts. Try these recipes with your students.

Peanut Butter

Shell 1 bag of salted peanuts. Then place 1 cup of shelled peanuts and 1 tablespoon of oil in a blender. Blend at high speed until mixed. Have the students spread the peanut butter on crackers or bread.

Peanut Butter Fondue Mix

1 cup of peanuts, 1/2 can of evaporated milk, 1/3 cup light brown sugar and 2 tablespoons of margarine over low heat—preferable in a fondue pot (if not, a saucepan). Provide an assortment of fruits and vegetables, e.g., marshmallows, banana chunks, strawberries, celery and fondue sticks. Tell the students to put their selections on the end of fondue sticks and dip them into the peanut fondue.

Note: Save shells from the peanuts and allow time for the students to make a peanut shell mosaic with them.

MANY MOONS

Author
James Thurber

Illustrator
Louis Slobodkin

Publisher
Harcourt Brace Jovanovich, Inc., 1943

Pages	Grade Level
45	K-3

Additional Books by Thurber
My Life and Hard Times; My World and Welcome To It; Thurber Carnival

Summary
Young Princess Lenore is ill, but she says she will be well again if she can have the moon. Her father, the king, engages all of his wisest men—Lord High Chamberlain, The Royal Wizard, and The Royal Mathematician—to find a way to get the moon for the princess. They tell the king that it cannot be done. It is the Court Jester who proposes that Princess Lenore be given a gold-shaped moon on a chain to wear around her neck instead. Everyone worries that the princess will become ill again when she sees that the moon is in the sky even though she has a moon on her necklace. But she is not upset and surprises them by explaining that the moon's reappearance in the sky is just like what happens when you lose a tooth and a new one grows in its place.

Introduction
Introduce children to *Many Moons* by telling them that they are about to hear the story of a princess and a wish she made. Open the book to the second page of the story and show children the illustration of Lenore in her bed. Ask children what the picture tells them about Lenore. (Answers may vary, but are likely to include observations that she seems to be very small, she lives in a grand place, she is wearing her crown even though she is in bed, etc.) Ask children why she might be in bed. After they have volunteered their explanations, show them the picture of Lenore and the plate of tarts (it is placed just before the title page). Ask if the picture gives them any clues. Once their curiosity is piqued, begin the story.

Key Vocabulary
Write the following words on the chalkboard and choral read them:

kingdom	princess	gold	wisest
moon	king	scroll	royal

Key Vocabulary Instruction
Write the vocabulary words on yellow construction paper cut into circles to represent the moon. Adhere the "moons" to the chalkboard with masking tape. Then write the following sentences on the chalkboard. Ask the children to choral read each of the sentences, select the vocabulary word(s) that fits into each sentence, and then ask one child to place the "moon shape" with the vocabulary word on the blank in the sentence. Choral read the sentence again.

The little princess, Lenore, wanted the _____.

The _____ was a beautiful little girl.

The princess' father was called a _____.

The princess and her father lived in a _____ palace.

A king is a ruler of a _____.

A _____ is paper that was rolled up and then unrolled for the king to read.

The king asked his _____ men for advice.

The princess was happy with her _____ moon necklace.

From *Read It Again! More Book 1*, published by Good Year Books. Copyright © 1991 Terri Christman and Liz Rothlein.

MANY MOONS

Discussion Questions

1 Why do you think the princess asked for the moon? Explain. (Answers may vary.)

2 Do you think the king was wise to tell his daughter that she could have the moon? Why or why not? (Answers may vary.)

3 Why was her father, the king, so determined to get her the moon? (He wanted her to get well again.)

4 Do you think giving the princess the moon could make her get well again? Explain. (Answers may vary.)

5 Who did the king call upon for help in obtaining the moon? (The Lord High Chamberlain, The Royal Wizard, The Royal Mathematician, and the Court Jester.)

6 Who, in this story, do you think was the wisest? Why? (Answers may vary.)

7 If you were called upon by the king to get the moon for the Princess, what ideas would you have had for him? (Answers may vary.)

8 Do you think Princess Lenore was happy now that she had "the moon?" Why or why not? (Answers may vary.)

Bulletin Board

In the story *Many Moons*, Lenore gets ill from eating too many raspberry tarts. Have the students think about something they like so well that, if permitted, they would eat too much of it. Once they decide, have them draw it on a sheet of 8 1/2" x 11" piece of white paper. Have them copy and complete this sentence below their drawing: I would like to eat too much _____. Label the bulletin board "Too Much..."

Special Notes about the Activities

Activity 2: Reread the descriptions of the moon offered by The Lord High Chamberlain, The Royal Wizard, The Royal Mathematician and Princess Lenore. Clarify words that are likely to be unfamiliar such as "molten" and "asbestos". Ask children to discuss what the moon is really made of. Once the factual description has been established, ask them to imagine themselves as the author of the story. How would they have had one of the characters describe the moon? After a period of discussion, distribute Activity Sheet 2.

MANY MOONS

**ACTIVITY
SHEET 1**

Directions
Below are many moons. Some of the letters of the alphabet
are on the moons and some are missing. Fill in the missing
letters. Don't forget to color the moons.

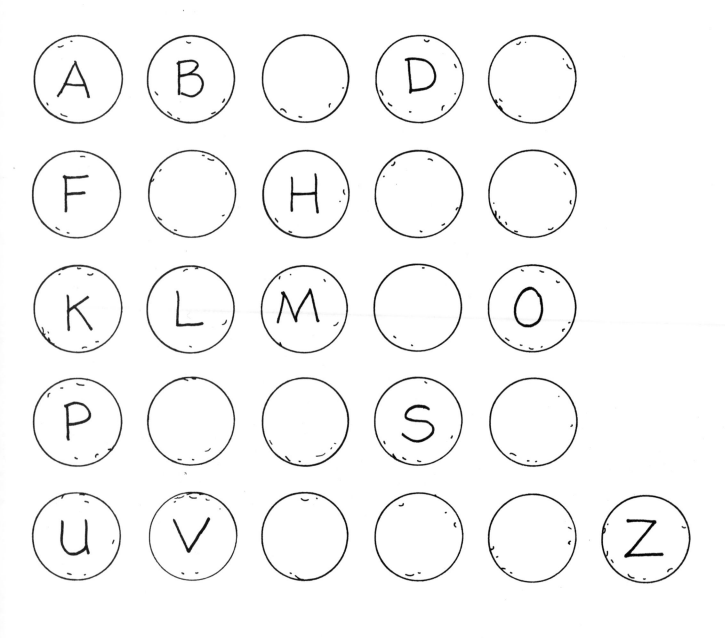

Count how many letters are in the alphabet. _____

From *Read It Again! More Book 1*, published by Good Year Books. Copyright © 1991 Terri Christman and Liz Rothlein.

Name_____ Date_____

**ACTIVITY
SHEET 2**

Directions
Below are four different descriptions of the moon. Read each
description and illustrate.

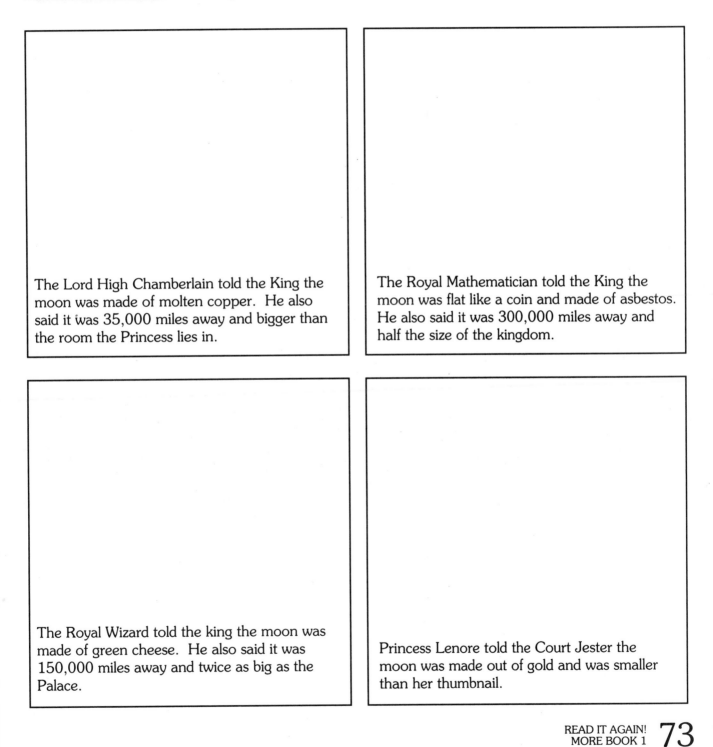

The Lord High Chamberlain told the King the
moon was made of molten copper. He also
said it was 35,000 miles away and bigger than
the room the Princess lies in.

The Royal Mathematician told the King the
moon was flat like a coin and made of asbestos.
He also said it was 300,000 miles away and
half the size of the kingdom.

The Royal Wizard told the king the moon was
made of green cheese. He also said it was
150,000 miles away and twice as big as the
Palace.

Princess Lenore told the Court Jester the
moon was made out of gold and was smaller
than her thumbnail.

Name_____ Date_____

Directions
Read the paragraph entitled "The Moon." Then read the
sentences below. If the sentence is true, put a <u>T</u> in front of it.
If the sentence is false, print <u>F</u>.

The Moon

The moon is a satellite of the earth. Because it is a satellite, the moon travels
around the earth. The moon is about 240,000 miles away from earth. The
moon is not as big as earth. The moon has mountains, plains, and hollows.
There is no air or water on the moon. The moon has day and night just as the
earth has, but each of its days and nights is as long as two of our weeks. During
the day the temperature drops below freezing. Gravity on the moon is much less
than gravity on earth. A person who weighs 90 pounds on earth would weigh
only 15 pounds on the moon.

_____ 1. The earth travels around the moon.

_____ 2. The moon is 24,000 miles from earth.

_____ 3. The earth is bigger than the moon.

_____ 4. The moon has mountains, plains, and hollows.

_____ 5. You could swim on the moon.

_____ 6. You could live on the moon.

_____ 7. The moon has days and nights.

_____ 8. The temperature stays the same on the moon.

_____ 9. The gravity on the moon is less than gravity on earth.

_____10. You would weigh more on the earth.

From *Read It Again! More Book 1*, published by Good Year Books. Copyright © 1991 Terri Christman and Liz Rothlein.

MANY MOONS

Additional Activities

1 Princess Lenore explained the presence of the moon in the sky again (after she had been given the moon to wear around her neck) as the same phenomenon as when a tooth falls out and a new one grows in its place, or when a flower is cut in the garden and a new one grows. Brainstorm with the student about other things that are replaced in such a manner. Make a list of these things on the chalkboard, e.g., leaves fall off a tree, new leaves appear; fingernails are cut, new ones grow; hair is cut, new hair grows.

2 Remind children of the characters in the story who presented long lists to the king. Tell them that they can make their own long lists. Either provide them with long strips of paper that can be written on and rolled up like a scroll or instruct them to use 8 1/2" x 11" white sheets of paper and tape or glue them together until they have a long sheet of paper (approximately four or six sheets put together). Show them how to roll the paper into a scroll. Then encourage the students to write about or illustrate the things they would want to have if they could have anything in the world. Provide time for students to share their scrolls with others.

3 Read *Papa Please Get the Moon for Me* by Eric Carle to the students. Help children compare and contrast this book with *Many Moons*. Talk about characters, setting, how the story begins and ends, etc. Ask children which story they like best and why.

4 Princess Lenore in *Many Moons* is always wearing her crown. Have the students design crowns on a sheet of white construction paper. They can glue on glitter, sequins, feathers, cotton, buttons, etc., to make their crowns unique. You may want to have a crown contest. Give a prize to the one that is most unusual, scariest, prettiest, etc.

An Extra Treat

Make Lenore's raspberry tarts with the students. To make them you will need to purchase packages of refrigerated dinner rolls (enough for each student to have one roll) and raspberry jam. Follow the cooking directions on the tube of dinner rolls except, before you bake them, have each student make a hole in the middle of his/her roll. This can be done by pushing the dough to the side. Once they come out of the oven, scoop a teaspoonful of raspberry jam in the center. Bon appetite!

MISS RUMPHIUS

Author
Barbara Cooney

Illustrator
Barbara Cooney

Publisher
The Viking Press, 1982

Pages	Grade Level
30	K-2

Other Books by Cooney
*Little Brother and Little Sister;
The Little Juggler. She has also
illustrated the books of many
other authors.*

Summary
As a young girl, Alice Rumphius decides she will go to faraway places and return to live by the sea when she is old. Her grandfather tells her that she must also do something to make the world more beautiful. When Alice grows up, she travels to tropical islands, faraway mountains, jungles, and finally to the Land of the Lotus-Eaters. Eventually, however, she comes back to the house by the sea. Alice settles on a way to make the world more beautiful; she plants lupine seeds all around her. The seeds blossom into beautiful blue, purple, and rose-colored flowers. She has made her world beautiful.

Introduction
Gather your students around you and ask them to look carefully at the illustration of Alice on her grandfather's lap. Then show them the illustration of Alice as an old woman, with children at her feet. Tell the students that the person who is in both illustrations is the character you will be reading about. Her name is Miss Rumphius. Ask the children to study each picture carefully (the comparison will be easier if you have two copies of the book). Challenge students to see how many things they can find that appear in both illustrations (e.g., the pictures on the wall, seashells, the curtains, the color of the walls, the presence of a cat, etc.) Ask them to find the things that are different, too. Then pose the questions: Do you think Miss Rumphius is in the same house in both illustrations? Why or why not?

Key Vocabulary
After the children have enjoyed the story, introduce some key words. Write the following words on the chalkboard and choral read them:

sea	ship	seeds	artist
island	lupines	garden	bird

Key Vocabulary Instruction
Give each student a blank sheet of 8 1/2" x 11" paper. Working together, have them fold the paper in half lengthwise once and then again. Next, fold the paper in half the other direction two times so that they have eight boxes. Number the boxes one through eight. The students should then write a vocabulary word in each box. Talk about each word with the students and then have them create an illustration in each box to represent the word. Allow time for the students to share their illustrations.

MISS RUMPHIUS

Discussion Questions

1 Describe some of the things Alice and her grandfather did together. (Answers may vary, but might include painting and sharing stories.)

2 What were some of the things Miss Rumphius did in the library? (She dusted books, kept the books from getting mixed up, helped people find the books they wanted, and read about faraway places.)

3 Which of the faraway places Miss Rumphius visited would you like to visit? Explain. (Answers may vary.)

4 Describe Miss Rumphius' house by the sea. (Answers may vary.)

5 When Miss Rumphius felt better she took a walk on the other side of the hill. There she saw a large patch of lupines. Why was she so surprised? (She had not planted seeds there. It was the wind or birds that carried the seeds from her garden.)

6 Why do you think Miss Rumphius felt so pleased about planting the lupine seeds? (Answers may vary but may include that she had made the world more beautiful.)

7 How was Alice like her grandfather? (Answers may vary but might include: they both liked to do art work, they both traveled to faraway places, they both lived by the sea, they both told stories, and they both made the world more beautiful.)

8 What is your favorite flower? Describe how it looks. (Answers may vary.)

Bulletin Board

Place the caption I WANT TO LIVE . . . on the bulletin board. Next, place a world map under the caption. Have the students place their name and where they would like to live on a 5" x 8" index card (they may want to create an illustration to depict where they would like to live) and place it on the bulletin board. Finally, provide pieces of yarn and stretch it from the location on the map to the card.

Special Note about the Activities

Activity 1: Tell children that you are giving them a picture of how the flowers in Miss Rumphius' garden might have looked. Ask them to follow the directions as they color the flowers. Encourage them to check off each direction after it is completed.

Name _____ Date_____

ACTIVITY
SHEET 1

Directions
Use these directions to color the flowers Miss Rumphius planted in her garden.

_____ 1. color 3 flowers blue

_____ 2. color 2 flowers yellow

_____ 3. color 1 flower red

_____ 4. color 4 flowers pink

_____ 5. color 5 flowers purple

_____ 6. color 4 flowers orange

_____ 7. color 1 flower any color

_____ 8. color the grass and leaves green

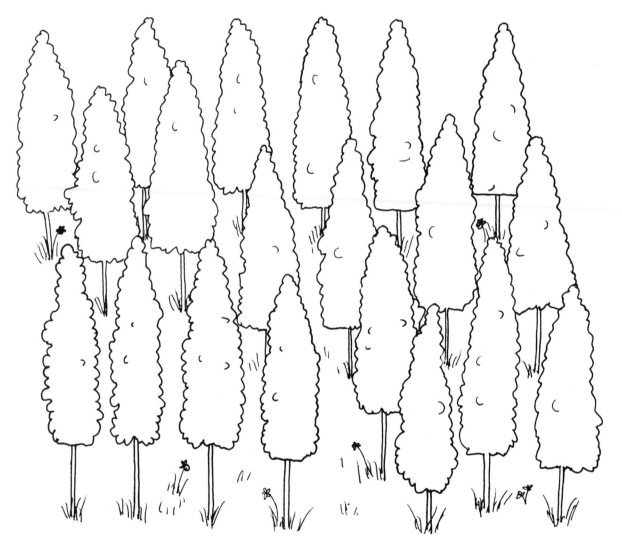

How many flowers are there in all? _____

Name_____ Date_____

Directions
Miss Rumphius hurt her back in the Land of the Lotus-Eaters
when she was getting off a camel. Let's make her a get well
card! Cut out the card below. Fold in half on the dotted line.
Decorate the outside and write a get well note on the inside.

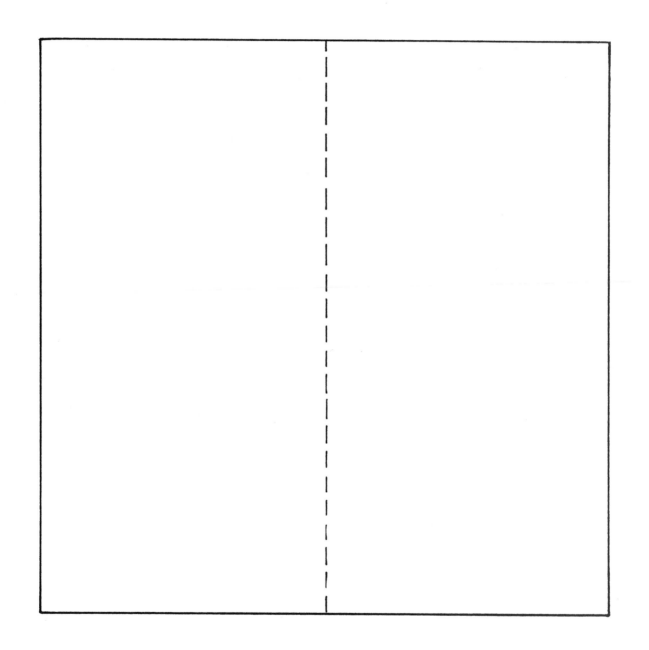

PETUNIA

Author
Roger Duvoisin

Illustrator
Roger Duvoisin

Publisher
Alfred A. Knopf, Inc., 1950

Pages	Grade Level
32	K-3

Additional Books by Duvoisin
A For the Ark; Day and Night; Jasmine; Our Veronica Goes to Petunia's Farm; The Four Corners of the World; Veronica; Petunia, Beware!; Petunia's Christmas

Summary
Petunia the goose finds something she had never seen before in the meadow—a book! She remembers hearing Mr. Pumpkin say, "He who owns books and loves them is wise." In this story, Petunia discovers that it is not enough to own and love books—you must be able to read them.

Introduction
Show the illustrations of Petunia looking at the book (a double-page spread near the beginning). Ask children to describe what they think is happening in these illustrations. What do they think Petunia is like? Is she curious? Afraid? What will she do with the book? Once children have made their predictions, read the story. Then recall their predictions. Were they right about Petunia or were they surprised?

Key Vocabulary
Write the following words on the chalkboard and choral read them:

goose	book	proud	wise
danger	silly	read	meadow

Key Vocabulary Instruction
Give each of the students a sheet of red construction paper. Fold it in half horizontally to make a book shape. Next ask them to color and cut out the goose pattern provided on page 83. Place it on the cover of the book. Place two folded sheets of 8 1/2" x 11" white paper inside. On each folded page, write a vocabulary word and pronounce it. Finally, as a class, write a sentence using each word. The students will now have their own book to read.

From *Read It Again! More Book 1*, published by Good Year Books. Copyright © 1991 Terri Christman and Liz Rothlein.

PETUNIA

Discussion Questions

1 Why did Petunia decide to take the book she had found? (She didn't want anyone to call her a silly goose.)

2 Why did the animals begin to ask Petunia for advice and opinions? (She carried a book and looked wise.)

3 Petunia influenced the farm animals in many ways. Which farm animal do you think was persuaded the most after she gave advice? (Answers may vary.)

4 Why do you think Petunia thought candies were in the box of firecrackers? (Answers may vary.)

5 Why did Petunia want to learn to read? (So she could be truly wise and make her friends happy.)

6 Petunia learned that it was not enough to carry wisdom around under her wing. She must put it in her mind and heart. What do you think these words mean? (Answers may vary.)

7 Why do you read? (Answers may vary.)

8 Describe things you have done that have made you feel proud. (Answers may vary.)

Bulletin Board

Place the caption, "Feeling Proud" on the bulletin board. Next, copy the goose pattern from the Key Vocabulary Instruction so that each child has a goose. Have each child place his/her name on the body of the goose. Also, give them a 5" x 8" index card. On the index card have them write and complete, I feel proud when I _____. They might want to put a small illustration on the bottom of the card. Have them attach the card to the bill of the goose and place it on the bulletin board.

From *Read It Again! More Book 1*, published by Good Year Books. Copyright © 1991 Terri Christman and Liz Rothlein.

Name_____ Date_____

Directions

Can you put the story back in order? Color the pictures and cut them out. Glue them on a new piece of paper starting with the picture that shows what happened first.

PETUNIA   Name_____ Date_____

Directions
Here is a picture of Petunia's barn. Cut out the barn and fold it
in half on the dotted line. The words "Big Barn Book Report"
should be written on the cover. Use the report to tell about
Petunia. Draw your favorite part of the story next to your
report.

A BIG BARN BOOK REPORT

By: _____

Title: _____

Author: _____

This book is about: _____

_____

_____

My favorite part is: _____

_____

_____

_____

PETUNIA   Name _____ Date _____

Directions

In the beginning of the book, Petunia felt very good about finding the book and helping her friends ☺. At the end of the book, she felt very bad because she didn't read the word on the box correctly and her friends got hurt ☹. Below are ten sentences. Read each of them carefully and decide how you would feel if these things happened to you. Color the happy face yellow if you feel happy about what the sentence says. Color the unhappy face black if you feel unhappy about what the sentence says.

ACTIVITY SHEET 3

☺ ☹   1. You can't find your homework.

☺ ☹   2. On Saturday you get to go to the movies.

☺ ☹   3. Your best friend is moving away.

☺ ☹   4. Tonight you can stay up late and watch TV.

☺ ☹   5. Before you go to bed tonight, someone will read you a story.

☺ ☹   6. You are going to go to a different school.

☺ ☹   7. Tomorrow you will get a haircut.

☺ ☹   8. You are going to have chicken for dinner.

☺ ☹   9. On your birthday, you will get a pet dog as a gift.

☺ ☹   10. You are going to get a new baby sister.

PETUNIA

1 Draw a rectangular shape on the chalkboard which will represent a book. Place the word *book* in the rectangle. Next, have the children give you one word that comes to mind when they hear the word *book*. For example:

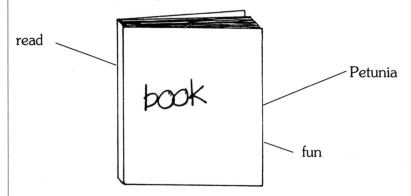

Then have the children combine their word with the word *book* in order to create a sentence. For example, Petunia found a *book*. Finally, have the children illustrate the sentences they have created. Share these sentences and illustrations as a group.

2 Discuss and list all the animals mentioned in *Petunia:* a pig, a rooster, a hen, a dog, a cow, a horse, a goat, a sheep, a turkey, a duck, and a goose. Provide the children with ink pads and white paper. Have them create these and other animals from their thumbprints. The thumbprints may be the head, body, etc. They can then add eyes, ears, noses, legs, fur, and other features to the thumbprints. Finally, have each child label their animal thumbprints.

3 Petunia affects the animals in many ways. Make four columns on the blackboard. In the first column, at the top, place the word *animal* and list all the animals Petunia affected. In the second column, write the word problem. In that column list each animal's problem. In the next column, put the word *affected* and list how each animal was affected by her advice and opinions. In the last column, write the words *our solution*. As a group, decide how you would have solved each animal's problem and place it in that column.

Example:

Animal	Problem	Affected	Our Solution
rooster	comb sore	sad	

From *Read It Again! More Book 1*, published by Good Year Books. Copyright © 1991 Terri Christman and Liz Rothlein.

PETUNIA

4 Talk with the students about the box of firecrackers in the meadow. Have them think about what else could have been in the box when the animals opened it and what would have happened to them. Provide the students with paper and ask them to draw a box. When they have decided, they should label it to tell what is inside. Next, have them write about what might happen when it is opened. Share these new endings aloud.

An Extra Treat
Have the students make some Petunia Oat Squares by following this recipe:

> 4 1/2 tbsp. butter or margarine
> 6 cups of small oat squares
> 6 tbsp. parmesan cheese
> salt, if desired

Melt the butter/margarine and pour it over the oat squares. Then sprinkle with parmesan cheese and mix well. Add salt, if desired. Finally, bake the mixture for 5 minutes at 350 degrees. Write the recipe on the chalkboard and allow time for the students to copy the recipe to take home.

THE RED BALLOON

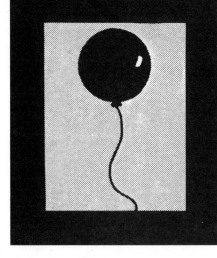

Author
Albert Lamorisse

Publisher
Doubleday, 1956

Pages	Grade Level
45	K-3

Additional Books by Lamorisse
No other books known by this author

Summary
In the story *The Red Balloon,* young Pascal is lonely. He doesn't have any brothers or sisters and his mother doesn't allow him to have any pets. One day he finds a red balloon on the way to school. The balloon is magical and the two become friends. They have fun and adventures together. When the balloon bursts near the story's end, Pascal has the biggest adventure of all.

Introduction
The story we are going to read takes place in Paris. Can anyone find Paris on this map (globe)? Can you think of any other stories that we have read that take place in Paris (e.g., *Madeline*)? Page through the book and show children some of the photographs. Ask: Can you tell from the photographs what Paris is like? Is it like where we live? Why (or why not)? How is it the same (different)?

Key Vocabulary
sky—space above the earth
balloon—round rubber bag filled with air
mother—female parent
boys—male children
principal—head of a school
window—an opening in the wall to let in air or light
magic—a mysterious happening
red—a color

Key Vocabulary Instruction
Using the balloon pattern provided, trace and cut out sixteen balloons from various colors of construction paper. Write one vocabulary word on eight of the balloons and the definitions provided on the others. Distribute the balloons to students (if possible, have them work in pairs). Pronounce and point to the first vocabulary word written on the chalkboard. Ask the student(s) who has the definition for the word to bring it to the chalkboard. If students do not recognize the definitions, discuss the meanings of the words and offer hints. Then tape the definition balloon next to the matching vocabulary balloon.

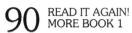
From *Read It Again! More Book 1*, published by Good Year Books. Copyright © 1991 Terri Christman and Liz Rothlein.

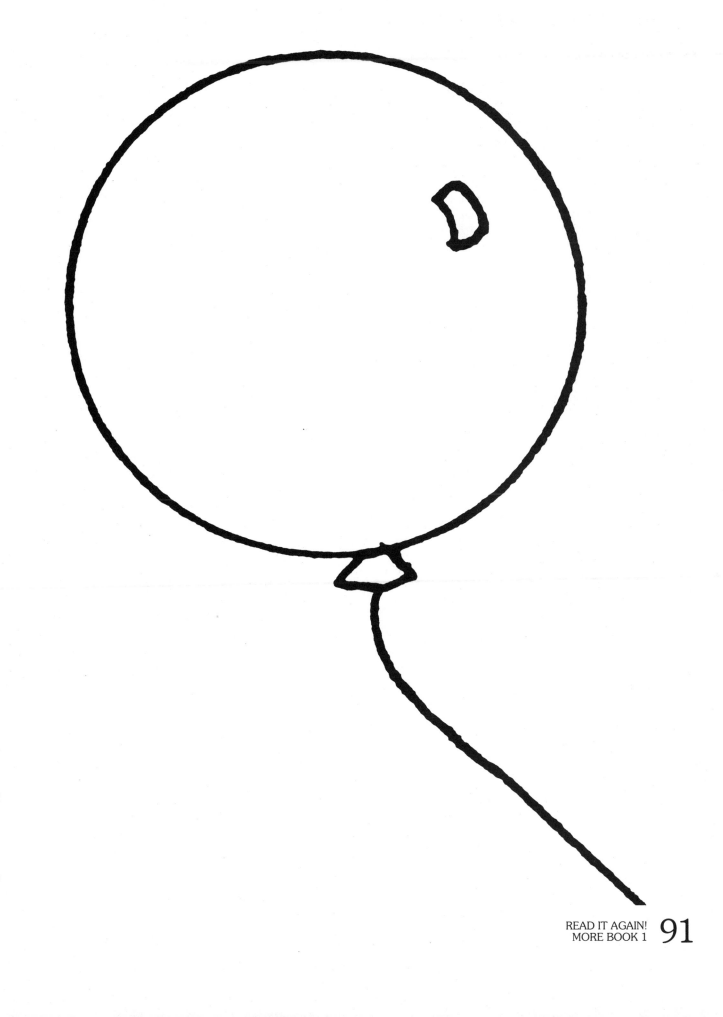

THE RED BALLOON

Discussion Questions

1 Do you think this story is real or make-believe? Why? (Answers may vary.)

2 Why did Pascal's mother throw the balloon out the window? (Because she found out that it was the balloon that made him late.)

3 Why do you think the balloon was so important to Pascal? (Answers may vary, but may include: because he was lonely and the balloon became his friend, or because the balloon was trained or had "magic.")

4 Do you think Pascal's balloon was a magic one? Why or why not? (Answers may vary.)

5 What did the balloon do while Pascal was in school? (Answers may vary, but may include: flew over the school, went to the Town Hall with the principal, stayed with the janitor, etc.)

6 How do you think the principal felt about Pascal's balloon? (Answers may vary, but might include: embarrassed, angry, frustrated.)

7 Why do you think the red balloon would not fly away when he saw the boys fighting with Pascal? (Answers may vary.)

8 How do you think Pascal felt about the boys who took away his balloon and finally broke it? Explain. (Answers may vary.)

Bulletin Board

Provide each student with an 8 1/2" x 11" piece of construction paper. Use a variety of colors. Ask each student to cut or tear a balloon shape from this paper. Next ask each student to use the balloon to illustrate or adhere a picture of something that could become Pascal's friend, taking the place of the broken balloon. Finally, ask the students to verbally share or write a short explanation of how and why what they have selected could become Pascal's friend. Write the following caption on the bulletin board: "Pascal's New Friend". Adhere the balloons to the bulletin board.

Special Notes about the Activities

Activity 3: Review with the children the letter to Pascal printed on Activity Worksheet 3. Ask them to imagine that they are Pascal and write a letter in return that answers the questions.

From *Read It Again! More Book 1*, published by Good Year Books. Copyright © 1991 Terri Christman and Liz Rothlein.

THE RED BALLOON

Name_____ Date_____

ACTIVITY SHEET 1

Directions

Make each balloon the same color as the word printed inside of it. Count how many there are of each color.

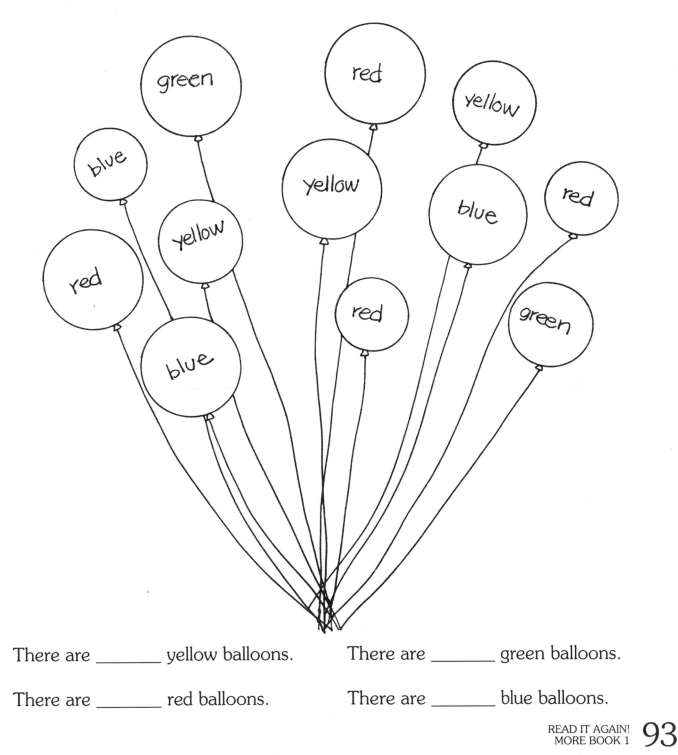

There are _____ yellow balloons.

There are _____ red balloons.

There are _____ green balloons.

There are _____ blue balloons.

Name_____ Date_____

**ACTIVITY
SHEET 2**

Directions
At the end of *The Red Balloon*, Pascal is holding onto the balloons as they lift him up into the sky for a trip around the world. In the boxes below, illustrate and/or write about what you think Pascal might have seen on his trip. Cut the boxes apart and staple them in the corner for your own story, "Pascal's Trip Around the World."

From *Read It Again! More Book 1*, published by Good Year Books. Copyright © 1991 Terri Christman and Liz Rothlein.

THE RED BALLOON

ACTIVITY SHEET 3

Directions

In the box below are some of the characters in the story. Read each sentence and fill in the blank with the correct character.

Pascal	janitor	gentleman
mother	teacher	girl
conductor	principal	

1. The _____ held a string to a blue balloon.

2. The _____ took Pascal by the hand and marched him out of school.

3. His _____ was angry when she found out that the balloon had made Pascal come home late.

4. The _____ did not allow dogs, large packages, or balloons on his bus.

5. The _____ was sweeping the schoolyard.

6. A _____ gave Pascal and the balloon shelter from the rain.

7. _____ found a red balloon tied to a street lamp on his way to school.

8. The _____ was surprised to see this strange new pupil (the balloon).

THE RED BALLOON

From *Read It Again! More Book 1*, published by Good Year Books. Copyright © 1991 Terri Christman and Liz Rothlein.

Additional Activities

1 Bring in a helium-filled balloon on a string. Have the children, one at a time, hold the balloon. As they are holding it, have them pretend the balloon will take them anywhere. Have them tell the class where they would like to go, why, and what they would see. They can illustrate where they would like to go and what they would see.

2 In this story, the balloon went to places where it was not allowed to go and Pascal had to tell it to stay out. Ask the children to tell you the names of these places while you write them on the chalkboard (the bus, the school, the church, the bake shop, etc.) Ask: Why do you think a balloon would not be permitted in these places? What problems would a balloon cause?

3 Write the word "real" in one column on the chalkboard and the word "make-believe" in another. Talk about what these words mean with children. Then, have them think of the many events in the story and for each one decide if it could have happened or if, instead, it was make-believe. Write down the children's words as they are offered. When complete, review the chart and read it together.

4 Have each student cut out a balloon shape from a wallpaper book. Glue a piece of yarn on the balloon. Group the balloons together on a bulletin board, wall, door, or chalkboard. It will look like a group of balloons that takes Pascal on a trip around the world.

An Extra Treat

Bring a watermelon to school. Slice the watermelon into 1" or 1 1/2" slices. Have the students, using a round cookie cutter, press out a round piece of watermelon. They can then place their round piece of watermelon on a popsicle stick. They now have their own red balloon to eat.

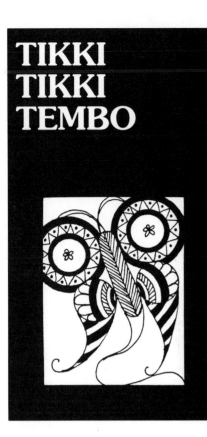

TIKKI TIKKI TEMBO

Author
Retold by Arlene Mosel

Illustrator
Blair Lent, Jr.

Publisher
Holt, Rinehart & Winston, 1968

Pages	Grade Level
43	Preschool-3

Additional Book by Mosel
The Funny Little Woman

Summary
Tikki Tikki Tembo is a Chinese folk tale about a young boy whose long name almost costs him his life.

Introduction
Tikki Tikki Tembo almost lost his life over his long name. His whole name was Tikki Tikki Tembo-no sa rembo-chari bari ruchi-pip peri pembo. Ask: Why do you think he had such a long name? Where do you think he lived? His name had a special meaning. Can you guess what it is? (After children have guessed, tell them that it means "The most wonderful thing in the whole world.") Then, ask children if they know what their names mean or where they come from. Bring in a name book which gives the meanings and origins of many names to share with children.

Key Vocabulary
Write the following words on the chalkboard and choral read them:

pumped	well	honorable	custom
son	rice	ladder	breath

Key Vocabulary Instruction
Using the butterfly pattern provided, cut out eight butterflies. Put the beginning letter of each vocabulary word on one-half of each butterfly and the vocabulary word on the other half. Cut the butterflies in half on the dotted lines. Distribute the letters and the words to the children. Next, ask them to move around and match the correct beginning letter with the vocabulary word beginning with that letter. Then ask the children to work cooperatively to pronounce the word and use it in a sentence.

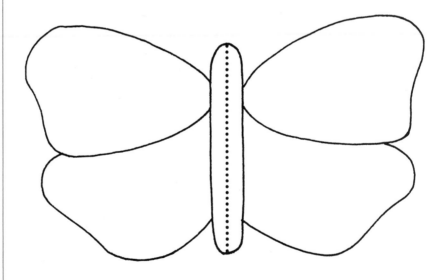

TIKKI
TIKKI
TEMBO

Discussion Questions

1 Why did Tikki Tikki Tembo's parents give him such a long name? (Because it was a custom in China to give the first born son a long name.)

2 Do you think Tikki Tikki Tembo's name was a good name? Why or why not? (Answers may vary.)

3 How do you think Tikki Tikki Tembo's brother Chang felt about having such a short name? (Answers may vary.)

4 Tikki Tikki Tembo's name almost cost him his life. What other disadvantages can you think of for having such a long name? What are some of the advantages of having such a long name? (Answers may vary.)

5 Why were the two boys playing at the well when Chang fell in? (Their mother was washing clothes in the stream nearby.)

6 Why did the mother send for the Old Man With the Ladder when each of the boys fell in the well? (Answers may vary but would probably be because he had a ladder to put down into the well.)

7 How do you think Chang felt toward his brother Tikki Tikki Tembo? (Answers may vary.)

8 At the end of the book we read, "And from that day to this the Chinese have always thought it wise to give all their children little, short names instead of great, long names." Do you believe that the Chinese gave up their custom of giving first-born sons a long name because of Tikki Tikki Tembo's accident of falling into the well? Why or why not? (Answers may vary.)

Bulletin Board
Put the following caption on the bulletin board, "My Name Looks Like . . ." Ask students to use the letters of their name to make a design that represents their name.

Example: Liz

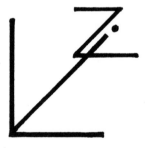

Ask students to create an illustration that represents what their names mean to them. For example, Tikki Tikki Tembo's name meant "the most wonderful thing in the world." Therefore, if Tikki Tikki Tembo was given this assignment, he would illustrate what he thought to be the most wonderful thing in the world.

From *Read It Again! More Book 1*, published by Good Year Books. Copyright © 1991 Terri Christman and Liz Rothlein.

TIKKI
TIKKI
TEMBO

Name _____ Date _____

Directions

In the boxes, draw two things about the place where Tikki Tikki Tembo lived that are different from where you live. You can get ideas from the story and the illustrations.

Name _____ Date _____

Directions

Help Tikki Tikki Tembo find all his names that are hidden in the Chinese Dragon below. When you find one of the names, circle it. The first one is done for you.

HIDDEN WORDS

Tikki Tikki	Tembo-no sa	rembo-chari	bari	ruchi-pip	peri	pembo

t i k k i t i k k i
e s p t r a c d f h
m j l n p q r s u r
b w y b d p e r i u
n e g i k m m o r c
o t u p e m b o v h
s x z a c e o g h i
a j l n p q c s u p
a w y b e g h i k i
c m o q s u a w x p
e z k n m o r p t s
g i q b a r i u r v

From *Read It Again! More Book 1*, published by Good Year Books. Copyright © 1991 Terri Christman and Liz Rothlein.

Name_____ Date_____

**ACTIVITY
SHEET 3**

Directions

Using the letters in Tikki Tikki Tembo's name as the beginning letters, make up names for other children. Write them on the blanks. They do not need to be real names. The first one is done for you.

T om _____

i _____

k _____

k _____

i _____

T _____

i _____

k _____

k _____

i _____

T _____

e _____

m _____

b _____

o _____

Select one of these names you like best. Draw a picture of what you think a person with that name might look like.

Name _____

TIKKI TIKKI TEMBO

Additional Activities

1 One of Blair Lent's illustrations in *Tikki Tikki Tembo* is a picture of the Chinese dragon. Have children look carefully at the illustration and describe the colors, shapes, and features they see. The Chinese dragon symbolizes good fortune as well as strength and wisdom. It is present at most celebrations, especially at the New Year's parade. The dragon is believed to keep the evil spirits away for the coming year. Provide students with a large sheet of paper, scraps of tissue paper, crayons, magic markers, etc. Ask them to create a Chinese dragon of their own.

2 Show the students the illustrations depicting Tikki Tikki Tembo's house and the other houses in his small village. Discuss how these houses look in comparison with where the students live. Provide the students with toothpicks, glue, and sheets of tagboard. Ask them to use the toothpicks to design their own Chinese house.

3 Provide or make rhythmic instruments. They could even include sets of chopsticks which are very inexpensive and can be purchased at most Chinese restaurants or food supply stores. As the story is read aloud, the students can tap out and repeat the rhyme of Tikki Tikki Tembo's name each time it is read in the story.

4 Introduce the students to other Chinese folktales, Mother Goose rhymes, etc. For example, present *Yen-Shen, A Cinderella Story from China* which is similar and yet very different from the more familiar version. Obtain books such as *The Fox That Wanted Nine Golden Tails* by Mary Knight; *The Magic Wings* and *8,000 Stones: A Chinese Folktale* by Diane Wolkstein; *The Weaving of a Dream* by Marilee Heyer; or Robert Wyndham's beautifully illustrated *Chinese Mother Goose Rhymes*.

APPENDIX

VOCABULARY

The following words are the key vocabulary words that are introduced and reinforced throughout this book.

angry	flowers	magic	seasons
appendix	food	mallard	second
artist	fourth	maple	seeds
	friends	meadow	ship
balloons		meal	silly
bears	garden	monkeys	sky
bird	giraffes	moon	spring
book	gold	mother	story
boys	goose	mouse	straight
breakfast	gun		son
breath		nest	summer
brothers	hatch	nicknamed	swam
	head		
caps	hippos	orchard	third
Chinese	honorable		tiny
city	hospital	pancake	town
country	house	pebble	tree
countryside		peddler	twelve
cried	imitate	policeman	
crow	island	princess	valley
cub		principal	village
custom	kill	proud	visitors
	king	pumped	voices
danger	kingdom		
dinosaurs		read	weather
ducklings	ladder	red	well
elephants	lines	rice	window
	lions	royal	winter
fall	lizard		wise
fifth	lonely	school	wisest
first	lupines	scroll	wood
flew		sea	
		seals	

From *Read It Again! More Book 1*, published by Good Year Books.   Copyright © 1991 Terri Christman and Liz Rothlein.

BOOK EVALUATION

Name of Book _____

Author of Book _____

Illustrator of Book _____

Color the face below that best tells what you thought about the book.

SUPER   GOOD   SO-SO   BORING   AWFUL

Who was your favorite character? _____

Why?_____

_____

Illustrate your favorite part of the story.

Name_____ Date_____

Directions
Attach the characters below and on the next page to tongue depressors. Use them to act out your favorite stories.

GENERAL ACTIVITY 2

Directions
Read each sentence carefully and follow the directions.

1. Color Johnny's bear brown.

2. Color the cap on the monkey's head blue.

3. Color Chibi's crow black.

4. Color Danny's dinosaur green.

5. Color Pascal's balloon red.

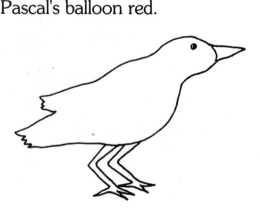

From *Read It Again! More Book 1*, published by Good Year Books. Copyright © 1991 Terri Christman and Liz Rothlein.

**GENERAL
ACTIVITY 3**

Directions
Draw a new cover for your favorite of the books we have read so far.

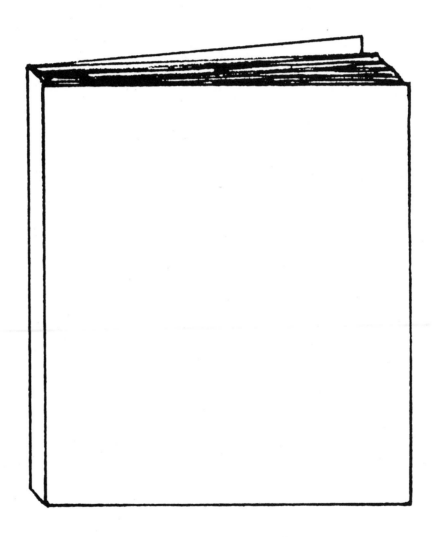

GENERAL ACTIVITY 4

Directions
Draw a line to match the titles of the books below with the main character of each book.

Danny and the Dinosaur

Caps for Sale

Alexander and the Wind-up Mouse

Petunia

Madeline

GENERAL ACTIVITY 5

Directions
Do the crossword puzzle by completing the sentences below.

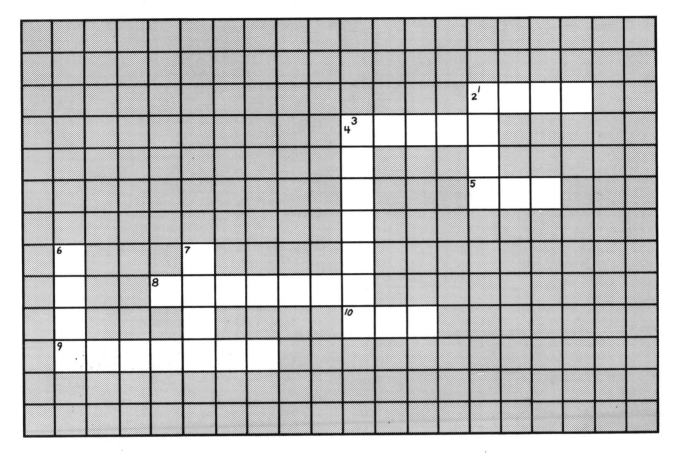

Across

2. Petunia found a _____.

4. Alexander was a _____.

5. Pascal's balloon was _____.

8. The little house like the _____.

9. Miss Rumphius planted _____.

10. One Chinese brother swallowed the _____.

Down

1. Johnny liked his big _____.

3. The _____ took the peddler's cap.

6. Tikki Tikki Tembo fell into the _____.

7. Lenore, the princess, wanted the _____.

Name_____ Date _____

Directions

Written on the book covers below are the main characters and the titles of the books. Find the main character that goes with each title and color the two that go together the same color.

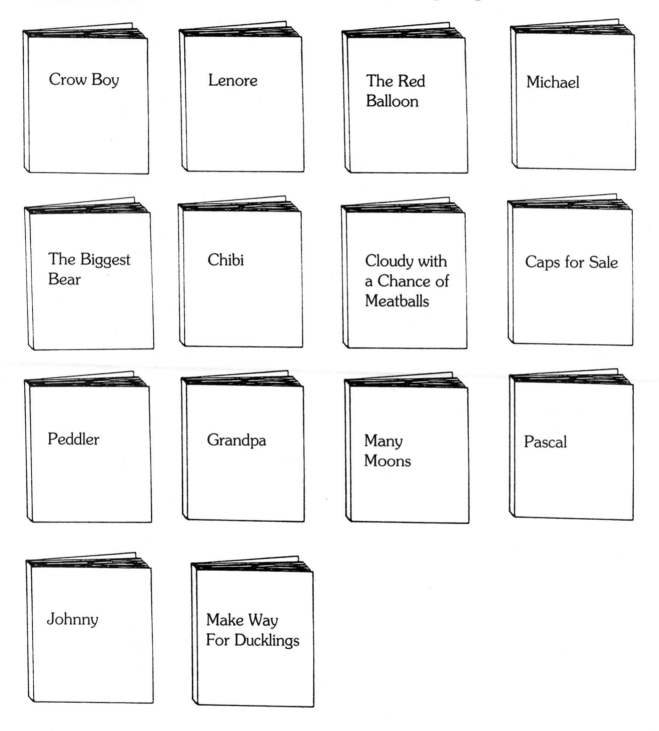

Crow Boy

Lenore

The Red
Balloon

Michael

The Biggest
Bear

Chibi

Cloudy with
a Chance of
Meatballs

Caps for Sale

Peddler

Grandpa

Many
Moons

Pascal

Johnny

Make Way
For Ducklings

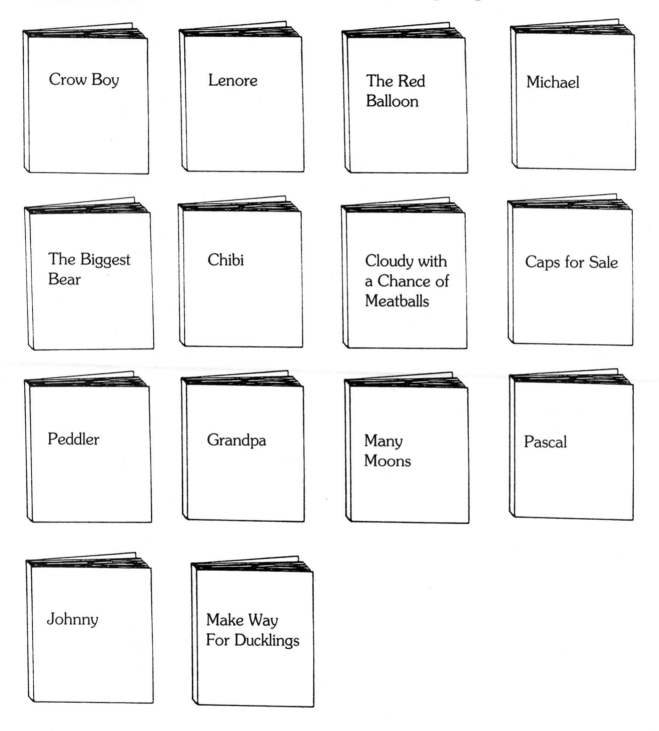

**GENERAL
ACTIVITY 6**

From *Read It Again! More Book 1*, published by Good Year Books. Copyright © 1991 Terri Christman and Liz Rothlein.

GENERAL ACTIVITY 7

Directions
Each of the flowers below has two leaves with a word written on each leaf. These two words belong to a particular book. Using the words from the box, fill in the blank on the flower with a word that goes with the other two words.

| peddler | bear | lines | crow | princess | goose | balloons |
| ladder | | | | | | |

GENERAL ACTIVITY 8

Directions
The setting is where and when a story takes place. In each of the boxes below, draw the setting for each story.

The Biggest Bear	*Crow Boy*
Petunia	*Tikki Tikki Tembo*

Name_____ Date _____

Directions
A fact is something that can be proven as true. For example, "Plants need water" is a fact. An opinion is something that cannot be proven true. For example, "All plants are beautiful" is an opinion. Read the following statements. Put an "F" in the blank if the statement is a fact. Put an "O" in the blank if the statement is an opinion.

GENERAL ACTIVITY 9

_____ 1. Pascal found a red balloon.

_____ 2. Tikki Tikki Tembo fell down the well.

_____ 3. The zoo was the best home for Johnny's bear.

_____ 4. The peddler sold caps.

_____ 5. The five Chinese brothers were clever.

_____ 6. The little house belonged in the country.

_____ 7. Petunia found a book in the meadow.

_____ 8. Madeline lived in Paris, France.

_____ 9. Danny's dinosaur was a good playmate.

_____ 10. Lenore wanted the moon.

_____ 11. Miss Rumphius made the world more beautiful because she planted flowers.

_____ 12. People screamed and threw things when they saw Alexander.

_____ 13. The people in Chewandswallow liked the food falling from the sky.

_____ 14. The children called Chibi names.

_____ 15. Michael was a wise policeman.

Directions
An antonym is a word that means the opposite of another word. Read each sentence below. Look at the underlined word in each sentence and locate an antonym, in the box, for that word. Put the letter of the antonym in the blank before each sentence.

ANTONYMS

a. lost	b. buy	c. city	d. day	e. dumb	f. small	g. nice

Example:___a___ Petunia <u>found</u> a book.

_____ 1. Johnny looked for a <u>big</u> bear.

_____ 2. The peddler wanted to <u>sell</u> his caps.

_____ 3. The five Chinese brothers were <u>smart.</u>

_____ 4. Lenore's moon came out at <u>night.</u>

_____ 5. The little house liked the <u>country.</u>

_____ 6. The boys were <u>mean</u> to Pascal.

From *Read It Again! More Book 1*, published by Good Year Books. Copyright © 1991 Terri Christman and Liz Rothlein.

Name ———————————————— Date ————————

GENERAL ACTIVITY 11

Directions
A synonym is a word that has the same meaning as another word. Read each sentence below. Look at the underlined word in each sentence and locate a synonym, in the box, for that word. Put the letter of the synonym in the blank before each sentence.

SYNONYMS

| a. glad | b. loved | c. lovely | d. ill | e. hated | f. shy | g. ocean |

Example: ___g___ The people in Chewandswallow sailed across the <u>sea</u>.

_____ 1. Chibi was a <u>quiet</u> boy.

_____ 2. Danny <u>liked</u> the dinosaur.

_____ 3. Madeline was <u>sick</u>.

_____ 4. Miss Rumphius planted <u>beautiful</u> flowers.

_____ 5. People <u>disliked</u> Alexander.

_____ 6. The Mallards were <u>happy</u> to find a home.

ADDITIONAL READ-ALOUD BOOKS FOR YOUNG CHILDREN

Allard, Harry. *Miss Nelson is Missing!,* illustrated by James Marshall. Houghton Mifflin Co., 1977.

Banks, Lynne Reid. *The Indian in the Cupboard.* Doubleday, 1981.

Brown, Marcia. *How Hippo!.* Charles Scribner's & Sons, 1969.

Brown, Marcia. *Once a Mouse.* Charles Scribner's & Sons, 1961.

Brown, Margaret Wise. *Goodnight Moon,* illustrated by Clement Hurd. Harper & Row, 1947.

Brown, Margaret Wise. *The Runaway Bunny,* illustrated by Clement Hurd. Harper, 1972.

Burton, Virginia Lee. *Mike Mulligan & His Steam Shovel.* Houghton Mifflin Co., 1939.

Carle, Eric. *The Very Hungry Caterpillar.* The Putnam Group, 1969.

Carle, Eric. *The Mixed-Up Chameleon.* 2nd Ed. Harper & Row, 1984.

Cohen, Miriam. *Will I Have a Friend?,* illustrated by Lillian Hoban. Collier Books, 1967.

DeBrunhoff, Jean. *The Story of Babar.* Random House, 1960.

De Paola, Tomie. *Nana Upstairs. Nana Downstairs.* Penguin, 1978.

DeRegniers, Beatrice Schenk. *May I Bring a Friend?,* illustrated by Behi Montesor. Atheneum, 1964.

Eastman, J.D. *Are You My Mother?.* Random House, 1960.

Freeman, Don. *Corduroy.* Viking Press, Inc., 1968.

Gag, Wanda. *Millions of Cats.* Coward, McCann & Geoghegan, 1928.

Geisel, Theodore S. (Dr. Seuss). *The Cat in the Hat.* Houghton Mifflin, 1957.

ADDITIONAL READ-ALOUD BOOKS FOR YOUNG CHILDREN

Heyward, DeBose. *The Country Bunny & the Little Gold Shoes.* Houghton Mifflin, 1939.

Hill, Eric. *Where's Spot?.* G.P. Putnam Publishing Co., 1980.

Hurd, Thacher. *Mama Don't Allow.* Harper & Row, 1984.

Johnson, Tony. *The Quilt Story,* illustrated by Tomie De Paola. G. P. Putnam Publishing Company, 1985.

Kantrowitz, Mildred. *Maxie,* illustrated by Emily A. McCully. Four Winds Press, 1970.

Keats, Ezra Jack. *The Snowy Day.* Four Winds Press, 1955.

Kraus, Robert. *Leo the Late Bloomer.* Crowell, 1971.

Krauss, Ruth. *The Carrot Seed,* illustrated by Crockett Johnson. Harper & Row, 1945.

Leaf, Munro. *The Story of Ferdinand,* illustrated by Robert Lawson. Viking Press, 1936.

Lionni, Leo. *Swimmy.* Pantheon Books, 1963.

Lobel, Arnold. *Frogs & Toads Are Friends.* Harper & Row, 1971.

Marshall, James. *George and Martha.* Houghton Mifflin Co., 1972.

Mayer, Mercer. *There's a Nightmare in My Closet.* Dial, 1968.

McCloskey, Robert. *Blueberries for Sal.* Viking Press, 1948.

McDermott, Gerald. *Anansi the Spider.* Holt, 1972.

McPhail, David. *Pig Pig Goes to Camp.* E.P. Dutton, 1983.

Minarik, Else Homelund. *Little Bear,* illustrated by Maurice Sendak. Harper & Row, 1957.

Ness, Evaline. *Sam, Bangs & Moonshine.* Holt, 1966.

Noble, Trinka H. *Jimmy's Boa Ate the Wash,* illustrated by Steven Kellog. Dial Press, 1986.

Numeroff, Laura Joffee. *If You Give a Mouse a Cookie,* illustrated by Felicia Bond. Harper & Row, 1986.

Parish, Peggy. *Amelia Bedelia,* illustrated by Fritz Siebel. Harper & Row, 1963.

Pinkwater, Daniel Manus. *The Big Orange Splot.* Hastings House, 1977.

ADDITIONAL READ-ALOUD BOOKS FOR YOUNG CHILDREN

Piper, Watty. *The Little Engine That Could,* illustrated by George Hauman & Doris Hauman. Platt & Munk, 1955.

Rey, H. A. *Curious George.* Houghton Mifflin, 1941.

Sendak, Maurice. *Where the Wild Things Are.* Harper & Row, 1963.

Spier, Peter. *Peter Spier's Rain.* Doubleday, 1982.

Steig, William. *Sylvestor & the Magic Pebble.* Simon, 1969.

Steptoe, John. *Mufaro's Beautiful Daughters.* Morrow & Co., 1987.

Ungerer, Tomi. *Crictor.* Harper & Row, 1968.

Viorst, Judith. *Alexander & the Terrible, Horrible, No Good, Very Bad Day.* Atheneum, 1972.

Waber, Bernard. *Ira Sleeps Over,* illustrated by Ray Cruz. Houghton Mifflin, 1972.

Wells, Rosemary. *Noisy Nora.* Dial Press, 1962.

Yorinks, Arthur. *Hey, Al,* illustrated by Richard Egielski. Farrar, Straus, & Giroux, 1986.

Zion, Gene. *Harry the Dirty Dog,* illustrated by Margaret Bloy. Harper &Row, 1956.

Zolotow, Charlotte. *Mr. Rabbit & the Lovely Present,* illustrated by Maurice Sendak. Harper & Row, 1962.

From *Read It Again! More Book 1,* published by Good Year Books. Copyright © 1991 Terri Christman and Liz Rothlein.

ANSWER KEY

Alexander and the Wind-up Mouse

SCRAMBLED WORD WORKSHEET

1. pebble
2. moon
3. lizard
4. magic
5. house
6. mouse
7. garden
8. friends

The Biggest Bear

SCRAMBLED WORD WORKSHEET

1. bear
2. woods
3. cub
4. orchard
5. maple
6. kill
7. gun
8. valley

ACTIVITY 1

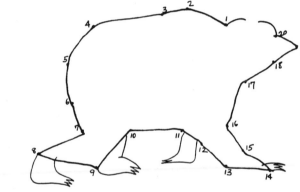

ACTIVITY 2

ACTIVITY 3

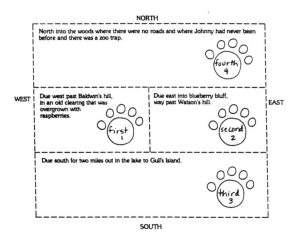

NORTH

North into the woods where there were no roads and where Johnny had never been before and there was a zoo trap.

fourth 4

WEST

Due west past Baldwin's hill, in an old clearing that was overgrown with raspberries.

first 1

Due east into blueberry bluff, way past Watson's hill.

second 2

EAST

Due south for two miles out in the lake to Gull's Island.

third 3

SOUTH

Caps for Sale

ACTIVITY 1

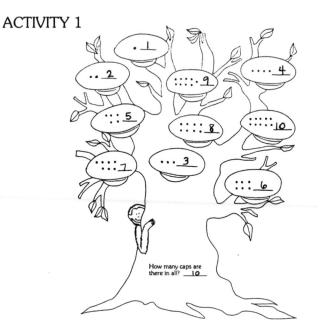

How many caps are there in all? 10

ACTIVITY 2

peddler   tree
head   monkeys
town   angry
country

Cloudy with a Chance of Meatballs

ACTIVITY 2

bedtime   downstairs   outside
everywhere   schoolhouse   nearby
whatever   townspeople   grandpa

From *Read It Again! More Book 1*, published by Good Year Books. Copyright © 1991 Terri Christman and Liz Rothlein.

ANSWER KEY

Crow Boy

ACTIVITY 1

4 crows
6 leaves

8 flowers
3 insects

ACTIVITY 2

The Five Chinese Brothers

ACTIVITY 1

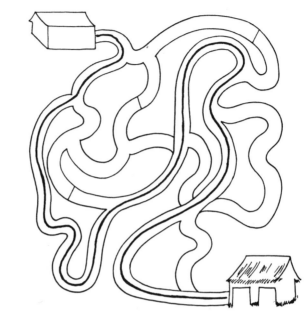

ACTIVITY 3

1. R	7. R
2. F	8. F
3. R	9. F
4. R	10. R
5. F	11. R
6. F	12. R

The Little House

ACTIVITY 1

ACTIVITY 3

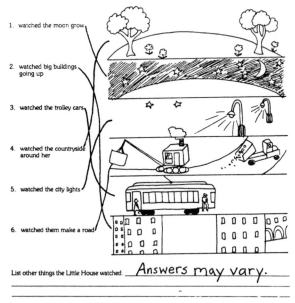

1. watched the moon grow
2. watched big buildings going up
3. watched the trolley cars
4. watched the countryside around her
5. watched the city lights
6. watched them make a road

List other things the Little House watched. Answers may vary.

ANSWER KEY

Madeline

ACTIVITY 1

sad	ice
bed	light
hours	line
door	by

ACTIVITY 2

Make Way for Ducklings

ACTIVITY 3

1. Mr. and Mrs. Mallard were looking for a place to live.
2. They thought they had found a place to raise their babies until a boy on a bicycle rushed by.
3. They built a nest in some bushes near the water.
4. Mrs. Mallard laid eight eggs.
5. The ducklings hatched.
6. Mrs. Mallard taught her ducklings how to swim, dive, walk in a straight line, and keep away from things with wheels.
7. Michael helped Mrs. Mallard and her ducklings cross the streets.
8. The Mallards lived happily on the island.

Many Moons

KEY VOCABULARY INSTRUCTION

moon	kingdom
princess	scroll
king	wisest
royal	gold

ANSWER KEY

ACTIVITY 1

C, E, G, I, J, N, Q, R, T, W, X, Y
26

ACTIVITY 3

1. f
2. f
3. t
4. t
5. f

6. f
7. t
8. f
9. t
10. t

Miss Rumphius

ACTIVITY 1

20

Petunia

ACTIVITY 1

The Red Balloon

ACTIVITY 1

3 yellow
4 red
2 green
3 blue

ACTIVITY 3

1. girl
2. principal
3. mother
4. conductor
5. janitor
6. gentleman
7. Pascal
8. teacher

ANSWER KEY

Tikki Tikki Tembo

ACTIVITY 2

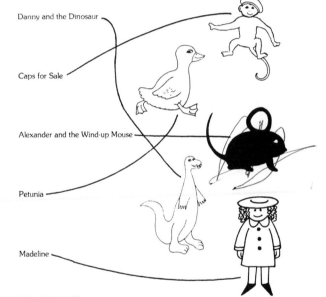

GENERAL ACTIVITIES

ACTIVITY 4

Danny and the Dinosaur

Caps for Sale

Alexander and the Wind-up Mouse

Petunia

Madeline

ACTIVITY 5

Across	Down
2. book	1. bear
4. mouse	3. monkeys
5. red	6. well
8. country	7. moon
9. lupines	
10. sea	

ACTIVITY 6

Crow Boy—Chibi
The Biggest Bear—Johnny
Cloudy With a Chance of Meatballs—Grandpa
Caps for Sale—peddler
Many Moons—Lenore
Make Way for Ducklings—Michael
The Red Balloon—Pascal

ACTIVITY 7

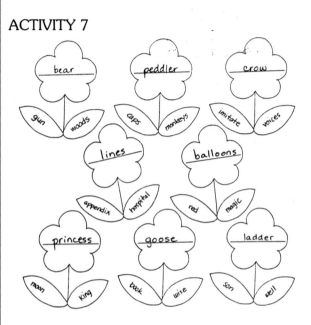

ACTIVITY 9

1. F	6. O	11. O
2. F	7. F	12. F
3. O	8. F	13. O
4. F	9. O	14. F
5. O	10. F	15. O

ACTIVITY 10

1. f	4. d
2. b	5. c
3. e	6. g

ACTIVITY 11

1. f
2. b
3. d
4. c
5. e
6. a